NORDIC INFLUENCE

ON

EMERSON'S SELF-RELIANCE

by

Elizabeth S. Scofield

Printed by:

Janaway Publishing, Inc.
732 Kelsey Ct.
Santa Maria, California 93454

2021

www.janawaygenealogy.com

ISBN: 978-1-59641-464-8
Library of Congress Control Number: 2021950403

Made in the United States of America

Table of Contents

"The most fundamental Viking-age belief was self reliance."

-Andrew Wawn, *The Vikings and the Victorians: Inventing the Old North in 19th Century Britain*

I came up with the original concept of the research topic in raw form in the summer of 1994; refined it and and wrote a proposal in the summer of 2002, and wrote the longer paper with original sources as evidence in August 2005. It has taken me all of this time to publish my findings. I tried a few times throughout the years all the way up until 2014, when I experienced some medical issues, at which time I put the bulk of the research away. Now I am very pleased to be able to present the research that I conducted all of those years ago in book form.

During the various trips to writing conferences in the years directly following my experience as a Ph.D. student, I shook hands and made contacts with several interested publishers, however there was an increasingly predictable stage during the discussions when the acquisitions editor simply did not know in which category to place the book. As one representitive from a publisher wrote in an email in July 2009, "Although we do publish works on Emerson, I'm afraid the Nordic mythology component takes it far enough afield…" The point was in his very polite email that his publishing house had decided not to publish the research because it wasn't mainstream enough at first glance. Now, the research is being officially presented for both recognition and for future researchers, and also as a base for my own future research. I have realized that there is still much to explore.

Recently, when I was re-reading the poem that Ralph Waldo Emerson wrote as a youth of 17 in the first book in the series of journals (Eds. Clark, George, Davis, Merrell, Gilman, William, Ferguson, Alfred *The Journals and Miscellaneous Notebooks of Ralph Waldo Emerson, Vol. 1 1819-1822*, The Belknap Press of Harvard University Press, Cambridge Massachusetts 1960),

I started reading the footnotes closely on that page and the pages both behind and in front of it, and noticed a book reference that I had not researched when I was a Visiting Associate at Harvard sixteen years ago. Everything is digitized now that wasn't back then. So, I took a chance, and looked it up.

On page 27 of the first printed journal volume,1820 *Wide World 1* (page 43 in the original handwritten journals), there stands a notation in the journal: <1> Liv. VIII of Buchanan's Scotland-Wallace x Valhalla x Archipelago x Paestum.

The book is written by George Buchanan, *History of Scotland*, 1690 (as is explained in the footnotes). I went to a search engine on the computer and typed in the information...and found a link to some pages in this very book from the British Library in the United Kingdom.

Here's the Link: ***The History of Scotland by George Buchanan, 1690 - The British Library (bl.uk)***
(The link displays 12 pages are available for viewing. - continue clicking the tab until page 208, then zoom in....and one can clearly read within the text on the screen... King of Norway, King of the Danes, Harold, Canute... It is all there. In a book that Ralph Waldo Emerson read during the years while he was still a student at Harvard.

My prose in this book, both past and present, is not perfectly written. However the research is solid, and can be confirmed with physical evidence that I collected a decade-and-a-half ago. More recently some of it can be verified with sources currently found online that were not widely available at the time that I was conducting this research. Perhaps I will publish all of the pages of evidence I still have in paper form at a later date. Today, I am happy to present my findings in this book and possibly in future volumes as well.

-Elizabeth S. Scofield

Portland State University

Portland, Oregon

1993

I graduated from the University of Portland with my Bachelor of Arts degree on May 2, 1993. After working full-time for three years following my final year of high school, I began studying at the university as a freshman when most people my age were entering into the first month of their senior year. Since I wanted to continue studying in a higher education program once I was done, I immediately thereafter applied to the Master of Arts program in English at Portland State University, and was able to enroll there the following September.

It was a difficult start at the time the program launched because my eldest stepsister had just been diagnosed with cancer for the second time. On top of this, I had recently begun a new job working part-time at a high-end portrait studio a few evenings a week, plus I had also decided to end my on-again, off-again relationship with a long-term boyfriend; he wanted to get married and I wanted to break up. Instead, I started a relationship with a college friend who got me through the winter of 1993-1994 and helped me not to return to the long-term boyfriend. Thank goodness! I was grateful.

In May 1994 (May 8, to be exact) my stepsister, Ellen, died of Non-Hodgkin's lymphoma. She actually died from pneumonia because her immune system was so weak from radiation and chemotherapy that when she contracted pneumonia, she simply never recovered.

After two weeks in a hospital room with an alarmingly quick and increasingly grim prognosis, the doctors held a conference with her parents, and disclosed to them that she was not going to get better. This was annihilating news. Within a few more days, it was time to let go, and we collectively stood in her hospital room, four of her family members, saying goodbye to Ellen.

That summer I wanted to continue taking classes at Portland State University in pursuit of my master's degree, to continue the momentum even though I was in shock and emotional pain. At this time, the master's program in English at Portland State University required students to specialize in three specific categories out of a variety of choices. The areas of focused study that I chose were 19th century English Literature, 19th century American Literature, and Women's Studies. I decided on these areas of interest because they occurred within the same 100-year time period, and much of the same information overlapped in each section, but from different perspectives. For example, the Industrial Revolution took place in both Great Britain and the United States at approximately the same time. Voting rights, women's suffrage movements, and other historical milestones mostly transpired between the years 1800-1900. In my view, it is one of the most riveting time frames in history.

Looking through the courses that were being offered for that summer in 1994, I found two courses that at first glance seemed rather appealing. One was a class about Ralph Waldo Emerson and the Transcendentalists, and the other was an unusual course that covered the topics of 'Goddesses, Myth, and History' taught by a visiting professor from Britain named Geoffrey Ashe. I begged my student advisor, Nancy Porter, to allow me to take this unique course. She quite literally put her head in her hands. "ONCE," she said, with a laugh, "I will allow you to take a class like this ONCE." I thanked her profusely, and immediately enrolled.

These two courses that I elected to take that summer happened to meet on the same days; one in the morning, and one in the afternoon. The Goddess, Myth, and History class was a bit off the main path in terms of how traditional university courses are often conducted; many guest speakers from local groups and organizations were scheduled to visit our class throughout the summer. More often than not, there was a lively discussion within the class after the guest speakers had finished their presentation to the students for the day. I frequently wondered how the next class was going to develop and unfold. It was really fun!

At some point during that summer, I began to notice parallel concepts that were being taught in both of these two courses. I learned in the Ralph Waldo Emerson class that he and the Transcendentalists conveyed through their lectures

and writings certain ideologies; specifically, that each
person is intrinsically connected to the earth, the
universe, and everything surrounding humankind. It
was taught in this class that each person should trust
his or her inner core, as this will allow the individual to
rely on oneself for intuitive guidance. Then, I would
attend the Goddess, Myth, and History class. In that
class, I learned that humankind is connected to the
earth's energies, and, simultaneously, all living things
are connected to one other in each their own way. For
example, I learned that trees grow in various directions
in accordance to other vegetation living near and
around them, evidence that plants communicate with
one another. It was pretty amazing to read about this
very same phenomenon in a scientific article years
later!

Each class day that summer I would sit in one
class taking place right after the other and think, "Huh,
that's a nearly identical concept to what I learned in the
other class." For several months, I attended these two
courses, back-to-back, during that summer in 1994 at
Portland State University. The parallels between the
doctrines, philosophies and ideals of the two classes
were so much along the same lines with each other
that I fully realized the similarities near the end of the
summer. This had to be more than just a coincidence.

Ultimately, near the end of the quarter, I approached the lecturer who taught the Emerson and Transcendentalists class and shared my reflections with him regarding the core themes of the two courses. I was at the time contemplating the possibility of writing a thesis, which in 1994, was not required for the master's program, but was permissible to the student if he or she pursued that path of choice and found an advisor to supervise the writing process. My professor listened to my observations about the concepts of what was being conveyed through each of the lessons as we stood in the doorway at the end of one class. He was pretty speechless by the correlation, and was surprised at the links, comparisons, and likenesses that I had made between the information presented in each of the two courses. We talked about it a little, and he said that he was fairly certain that a comparison between the two themes in an academic paper had not been done before. The one phrase I remember that he said from that conversation: "That's not a master's thesis; that's a thesis for a Ph.D." I smiled at him. He was a good teacher, and I was grateful for his encouragement. His words stayed with me.

The summer session ended, and I started my classes for the autumn quarter in the graduate program at Portland State University in September 1994.

The death of my stepsister, by this time, was slowly sinking in and affecting me in ways that I had not anticipated. I began to lose that core iron strength that I had always counted on for my success in academics; namely, that solid determination to finish a project, and finish it well. This trait had helped me through every academic milestone thus far in my life, and it was slowly subsiding. I was at a loss as to how to proceed. I started to fall behind academically, and it worried me.

That autumn quarter I was also enrolled in one of the most difficult courses of the program. We were required to learn all of the research methods within the brick-and-mortar physical compounds of the Portland State University library (this was, of course, before modern day internet was widely available). Deciding that I needed to resolve my dilemma as soon as possible, I made appointments with my professors and my supervisors; it was collectively agreed that I should take an incomplete grade for my classes that quarter, and finish them up the next quarter. I realized what I really needed was some time away to emotionally heal, so that I could, in fact, graduate with my degree.

So I started searching for a way to make that happen. Fortunately, I discovered a four-month German intensive language program taking place in Tübingen, Baden-Württemberg, Germany, during the next spring quarter in 1995. At this time, the state of Oregon was lending funds to various graduate students who needed additional financial support to complete parts of their education. Since one of the requirements for my master's program was to pass a foreign language proficiency level before the degree could be completed, I thought this might be a good solution. Thankfully, I qualified within the scope of this foreign language requirement for some of these graduate student loans. With renewed hope and energy, I applied to the German intensive program, and was promptly accepted. This inspired me to begin to get things organized and squared away, and to catch up. This was the emotional boost that I had needed.

Between January and March of 1995, I finished the coursework for the incomplete classes, located a friend who needed a new living situation to take my place in the house I shared with three other roommates, and put some items of sentiment into a storage unit. I also found a place to store my car. Such a relief! The departure date for Europe was scheduled for March 1995, and I had planned to stay in Germany to study for about 4 months. Unfathomably, I ended up staying for four-and-a-half years.

Roskilde University

Roskilde, Denmark

2001

The extended time that I spent in Germany was absolutely the best decision I could have made. This is especially true since I returned for one more year to Southern Germany a few years later. The first six months after arriving in 1995 were spent in Tübingen, located in the southwest part of Germany. This was followed by four years in Konstanz, a town on Lake Bodensee which shares a border with Switzerland. I met wonderful people from all over the world, many of whom are still friends of mine to this day. Plus, I was able to finish my master's degree in English by taking three extra classes at the University of Konstanz and transferring the credits back to Portland State University, which they thankfully allowed me to do. Additionally, I gained some teaching experience by working as an English as a Foreign Language Instructor at the University of Konstanz, the University for Applied Sciences, and also at a private in-town language school, the Sprachendienst, as well.

I was happy there, and even considered staying much longer in Germany if possible, still intending to somehow pursue the topic of comparing/contrasting Ralph Waldo Emerson's doctrines to pagan religious beliefs as a topic for a Ph.D. dissertation. Yet I was also inspired to look for a different program elsewhere in Europe instead of Konstanz for a new perspective.

Konstanz would always be a home to me, but by then I was ready to try somewhere new.

It turned out to be a little daunting to research possible Ph.D. programs in Europe. I wasn't certain at first where I wanted to go, however it was important to me for the place to be a good fit both academically and culturally. Finally I decided upon Roskilde University in Denmark. I liked the description of their programs, and my intent was to be admitted into their one year international program while preparing to apply to their Ph.D. program the following year. Their admissions team received my application, and thought my plan was a little unusual, but they liked it and sent the approved acceptance letter to me in the spring of 2001. I was absolutely thrilled, and very much looking forward to the start of a new adventure! At the end of that final semester in Konstanz, I finished up my work, handed in my apartment keys, packed up and drove a rental car from Konstanz, Germany to Copenhagen, Denmark in late summer of 2001. It was quite a journey.

Arriving in Copenhagen was intimidating and exhilarating all at the same time. Finding an apartment in the city was challenging, but I finally settled into one and got acclimated into the international program, getting to know my new classmates.

The first semester was spent learning about Roskilde and life in Denmark. It was during the second semester that I began to look for an academic advisor to supervise my dissertation for the Ph.D. application, and I chose to ask one of my professors from the international program, Dr. Dan Charly Christiansen, because I respected his style of teaching and admired his perspective on history. When I explained my idea for a dissertation topic, he listened patiently, and he agreed that it would make a good dissertation subject. He gave me one condition, though, for this area of focus: That I should find something specifically relating to pagan religion in Scandinavia. If I could find indisputable proof that Ralph Waldo Emerson knew about and utilized pagan stories from the Scandinavian countries, and specifically to focus on philosophies and religion from Denmark instead of full-blown widely found ancient European pagan religions (since this study would be conducted at a Danish University), then he would sign the papers from the History department to be my supervisor. That sounded fair to me.

So from then on, I started to read as many Ralph Waldo Emerson's published essays as I could find in chronological order at the Roskilde University library. Starting with the well-known essay "Nature",

12

I continued to read Emerson's published volumes, looking for clues and hints of Nordic culture. Finally I picked up the bound book of *English Traits*, published in 1856. There, between the pages, appeared quite a number of passages mentioning Odin, Northmen, Danes, Norway, Sweden, Scandinavians, and more! I couldn't wait to show Dan Charly what I had found. I still have this vivid memory of knocking on his office door, and, beaming with happiness, showing him the evidence of what I had discovered within the manuscript of *English Traits*. He smiled broadly, said congratulations, told me to research, design, construct and write up a proposal for the Ph.D. program application, and he would sign on as my supervisor. Hurrah!

All was bliss until a few days before the deadline for submission. The clerk in the History department called me and said they liked my application, but I could not apply to the Ph.D. program for History since my master's degree was in English. No one in the History department had noticed this minor but important detail until the last minute! I was then told I could apply for the English department Ph.D. with a February 2003 start date, six months from then, and my new supervisor would be assigned from the English department. Dan Charly Christensen apologized profusely for the History department's administrative mix-up, told me it was a good and innovative proposal, and that he was confident that it would be accepted. Taking a deep breath, I agreed to these terms, and arranged to take a few more classes for the upcoming semester while waiting for the process of the application to take its course. Thankfully, this plan worked. In November 2002, I was officially admitted into the Ph.D. program in the English department at Roskilde University beginning at the start of February 2003.

I often wonder if my academic career would have turned out differently if Dr. Dan Charly Christiansen had in fact been my supervising advisor during my Ph.D. candidacy. All of these years later, and thinking of him now, I hope he is well. He was a great help in what became the discovery of a lifetime.

After I had been accepted into the English department's Ph.D. program, two new supervisors, Dr. Ebbe Klitgaard and Dr. Soren Schou, were assigned to advise me. I didn't know what to expect since I had just met them, but I was filled with hope and optimism, having just started the program. My goals were to conduct original and beneficial research, and to form a successful academic collaboration with my supervisors going forward. I was hoping both goals were possible.

My two supervisors were quite supportive and enthusiastic for my project. Initially, I was encouraged to go to the Roskilde University library, check out as many books as I could possibly read about Ralph Waldo Emerson and the Transcendentalists, and to systematically prepare my first paper to hand into them for evaluation. With a narrowed focus and solid tangible subject matter, I was totally motivated to research this topic that I had wanted to pursue in general form for over a decade. Now, it had a format specifically involving Ralph Waldo Emerson's use of Scandinavian folklore, philosophy, history, and Viking trade routes as well as their cultural beliefs and norms that were all included in the collection of published essays within the volume of *English Traits.* At the beginning, I was so eager to begin work towards the Ph.D. that I didn't think much about anything else. The focus for the topic was slowly coming together.

One aspect was unforseen; the design and format of the Ph.D. program turned out to be more challenging to navigate than I had anticipated. It never occurred to me before starting to compare how an American program is managed and systematized with the workings and organization of a European program. An American program is often a blend or merge of a master's degree and Ph.D. degree combined. Many European bachelor's programs are five-year programs, effectively combining an undergraduate degree with a master's degree.

The European Ph.D. programs often expect students to have some life experience under their belt before they begin any sort of extensive graduate level study. I was certainly qualified for the Roskilde University Ph.D. program, meeting their entry requirements; however, it did not occur to me to inquire how it all processed from start to finish. I simply trusted that it would all work out. An American Ph.D. program directs the students to attend classes during the first few years and to participate in various conferences during this initial period of learning as well. This prepares the students for the next stage of the program, which is writing the dissertation. There is a reason why the unofficial "ABD" (All But Dissertation) term exists in the United States (and probably under different terminology in other countries as well). The writing of a dissertation is an entirely different experience than what transpires when taking courses. Most students agree it is a difficult endeavor to accomplish and complete, and some never finish. Other students finish with a flair and lots of academic accolades.

Additionally, during the course of a higher educational experience, some students become familiar with writing a quite lengthy paper before writing a dissertation; they either finish their bachelor's degree with a senior thesis in order to earn that degree, or they write a thesis as part of the requirement to graduate from their master's degree program. I had somehow managed not to have experienced either of these in my academic career thus far. Writing a thesis had not been required for either my undergraduate or my master's degree, even though, originally, it had been my plan to write a thesis for my master's degree, as mentioned previously. I had even gone to the lengths of obtaining an agreement from a faculty supervisor and was all set with a signed letter to present to the English department chair at Portland State University. However, because I wanted to stay in Konstanz, Germany a little longer, it simply made more sense to take the three extra classes instead of writing a thesis at the University in Konstanz. Therefore, by the time I had been accepted into the Ph.D. program at Roskilde University, I was quite accustomed to writing long documents, but had very little experience in writing a document that was equivalent to one of "thesis length". The long papers produced by the student groups during my time spent in the international program at Roskilde were more focused on the research, group dynamics, and delegation of tasks during the extended projects as part of a group, and not as much as a lengthy writing project produced by individual students. When entering the Ph.D. program at Roskilde, I was unfamiliar with how their doctorate program would progress and proceed.

So, perhaps naively, when I began writing papers for the Ph.D. degree at Roskilde, I felt very confident and optimistic. I later found out that my supervisors had been expecting a different type of structural format for most of the papers that I submitted. I was so happy conducting the research and self-assured with my many years of past successes in academic writing that it did not occur to me that my submitted assignments would be deemed as less than acceptable to them. That was a surprise. It was also a surprise that it happened not once, but quite often.

After I officially started the Ph.D. program, one of my first assignments was to write an overview of Ralph Waldo Emerson's manuscript *English Traits*, which I submitted to my supervisors in April of 2003. The purpose of this first paper was to provide a basic level summary of that volume of lectures in order to clarify what I wanted to explore going forward in this study. In the first few pages of the paper, I pointed out that Ralph Waldo Emerson delivered the lectures in the book during his trip to England in 1847-1848. He had traveled on the invitation of Mr. Alexander Ireland to give a series of lectures at the newly-unionized Mechanics' Institutes located in England and Scotland beginning in October 1847. After the lecture series was completed, Emerson

18

continued to deliver these same lectures to American audiences upon his return to the United States in mid-1848. He did not publish them as a collection until 1856.

There were many questions that I wanted to answer: Why specifically was he invited to the Mechanics' Institutes? Was he directed or instructed to include the characteristics of the Vikings in his lectures to the British audiences or was that his own decision? Why did he continue to give these lectures written for a British audience to American audiences once he had returned to the United States in 1848? Was it because Americans at the time wanted to know more about the British Victorian mindset? Most importantly, I wanted to find out from where and from whom Emerson had first learned about the stories of the Viking Age Scandinavians. It was important to know the reason for his use of both their mythology and their historical activities in his lectures for this series. Was he using them to supplement his points because he really admired them, or was it merely as an advertisement since the Vikings' myths and stories of exploration were experiencing a surge of popularity in 19th century Britain at the time? I focused on this last question going forward for some time during my studies. In my opinion, this was a key question.

That first paper that I submitted to my supervisors in April 2003 was generally well-received, with instructions from both of them to polish my writing style and to identify a framework for the writing for future papers. Neither of my supervisors were Emerson experts (fully admitted to me by Soren Schou in an email) yet it was pointed out that these facts and ideas about the Scandinavians historically being global adventurers were somewhat widespread during the 19th century, and Soren Schou wondered what set Emerson apart in this thinking. It was a fair question. I had at least a partial answer to that question many months later.

In an attempt to find answers to some of the other theories that I had, I began reaching out to a few people that I felt might know the answers to several of those questions, or at least point me in the right direction of where to search next. Since Ralph Waldo Emerson's journals were kept in Houghton Library at Harvard University, I felt it would be logical to reach out to one of Harvard's foremost experts on Ralph Waldo Emerson, Dr. Lawrence Buell. In May 2003, I wrote an inquiry email to him, which included the following research plan (NOTE: the dates regarding the Viking Age in my initial email sent to Dr. Buell are incorrect, since the recognized date of the Viking Age began with a raid on Lindisfarne just off the coast of England in the year 793, and ended just after 1050, with some experts declaring 1066 as the agreed-upon end date):

> Specifically, what I want to do is trace the influence of the Nordic mythology on Emerson, from when he was writing along with the general thought that the strength of the English came from the Scandinavian Vikings who raided their country 850-1100, to after his trip when he was writing his
> lectures based on his own experience with the English after his 6-month lecture tour in England 1847-48. My primary question to you is, how does one find lectures that he delivered that have not been published? in 1835 he gave a ten-lecture course where he used Sharon Turner's The History of the Anglo-Saxons -- are there any primary-source remains of those lectures?
>
> There are of course dozens of other questions I have, but I am hoping you will have the time and interest to answer this one.

Sharon Turner, a 19th century English historian, wrote extensively about his beliefs regarding the Norse impact on the Victorian English population. What I discovered much later was that Emerson not only read Sharon Turner when he was a student at Harvard, but also wrote about him in his journals. The major significance of this at the time was unanticipated.

Dr. Buell graciously answered my email the next day. His reply was kind and filled with suggestions for further research, including some writings by Dr. Phillip L. Nicoloff (with whom I corresponded directly 18 months later). Taking Dr. Buell's suggestions to heart, I followed up on what he had written in his email. I also started to do a bit more research of the Viking Age itself, including an in-depth reading of the *Edda*, and the *Heimskringla: History of the Kings of Norway* (written by 13th century scribe Snorri Sturluson in Iceland), and found some texts that outline some of the Viking Scandinavian beliefs and values of conduct from that time. Corresponding briefly once more with Dr. Buell in October 2003 regarding another Ralph Waldo Emerson question, he once again responded promptly with another kind suggestion for additional sources. This proved to be quite helpful.

So, pulling all of my efforts together to try to move my findings forward, in late November 2003 I sent an email to my supervisors attempting to formulate something more tailored with the research that I was conducting while detailing specific examples of the life of Ralph Waldo Emerson during his childhood. I outlined that Ralph Waldo Emerson's father had died when he was eight years old, his mother and aunt then decided to take in boarders in order to financially support their family, and at one point Ralph Waldo Emerson and his brother had shared one winter coat between the two of them. As a young man, Emerson fell in love with his first wife, who died a few years afterwards from tuberculosis. He then made plans for a trip and toured Europe for some months in 1833.

This email addressed to my supervisors was by no means formally written, simply a thread of my thoughts trying to find the connections through Emerson's own personal history and what he then introduced into his lectures. On the front page of my email, I wrote the following thoughts in regards to Ralph Waldo Emerson to my supervisors:

No one is more of an expert on how to live someone else's life than that person himself. This, in essence, is what formed the basis of Transcendentalism. Every

person simply needs to listen to
the inside of themselves, and the
right answer to whatever question
might be will [sic] appear. This in
turn, leads to the same concept,
but under a different name- Self-
Reliance. Because each person
has the correct answer to their own
lives, he or she doesn't need to
rely on others for answers, or help-
each person can rely on,
surprisingly, themselves, Do not
look outward for guidance,
Emerson preached-look inward.

Later I offered a few reasons why Ralph Waldo
Emerson may have used the stories of the Viking Age
Scandinavians and the written stories of the *Heimskringla*
and the *Edda* to help demonstrate his points and
thoughts to his audience but also to himself. I was
recognizing something that was coming through my
research which reminded me of that same "Eureka!"
moment that I had experienced at Portland State
University in the summer of 1994. Hinting at this, I ended
my email with the following sentence, "In one lecture,
Emerson states that this would be the highest of
situations, the meeting of two perfectly-balanced self-
reliant people."

This is where the development of my thoughts regarding my thesis topic began to fix upon, formulate, and focus. It seemed like a very good basis to have this all written out and to explain where I was planning to take the direction of the study, and possibly the next stage of my research approach as well.

While considering all of this, I traveled during the winter academic break that year in 2003 to meet my family on holiday in London, and also to prepare a document for my supervisors to evaluate upon my return to Denmark. Specifically, they were expecting a written analysis using current published studies comprised of other scholars' opinions and research on this topic. Until then I had been having difficulty finding very much at all in terms of other academics' published opinions, scholarly or otherwise, on Emerson and his use of Nordic Mythology no matter which places I searched, and no matter which assorted methods I administered. While in downtown London I picked up a few books at a Wiley-Blackwell bookstore, however I could find very little comparing Ralph Waldo Emerson and anything regarding Viking Age Scandinavians within the same written source. It was exasperating, though I did the best I could with what I could find. The works I collected for that paper included writings by Barbara Packer, Heather O'Donoghue, Robert Burkholder, and Phillip L. Nicoloff, to name a few.

I also compared writers from the 19th century who were known to be Scandinavian Viking experts, such as Samuel Laing. There were authors who evaluated each other's writings and points of view at the time over a hundred years ago. All in all, I felt I had written a fairly decent paper considering I was unable to locate many contemporary writers for a scholarly analysis with the narrowed focus for the topic, so when I returned to Denmark, I handed it in for review.

My supervisors, however, were not that pleased with this paper. It still did not contain the works of other current scholars on this particular subject. In an email from them dated January 27, 2004, my submitted paper was declared "a major step forward, although it is also clear that you still have something to learn about the level demanded for a Ph.D." This was incredibly disheartening to read and to hear being expressed. Whatever I was doing incorrectly, I wanted to fix, and yet I felt that I had very little direction from my supervisors regarding how to go about doing so. It was quite frustrating.

During the next month I had a completely different pressing topic to think about; specifically, which university I should attend for a 6-month study abroad experience, as was stipulated in the curriculum of the Roskilde Ph.D. program. My most logical options were to possibly attend

a university in Norway to study the origins of the book
Heimskringla: History of the Kings of Norway (even
though, as previously mentioned, the stories were written
down by the Icelandic scribe Snorri Sturluson), or attend a
university in England and trace the lecture route Emerson
took while he was delivering his Mechanics' Institutes
series of in-house orations during 1847-1848; or, ideally, I
could travel to Harvard University and study the original
handwritten journals of Ralph Waldo Emerson since they
were being kept at Houghton Library. All of these options
seemed like good uses of my academic time, regardless
of which choice I made.

Meanwhile I was also still trying to answer how and
when Emerson was first exposed to the stories of the
Scandinavian Vikings, and by whom. I found some
research on this matter that had been conducted by other
scholars, arriving at no definitive conclusion. Some
sources stated it was probably from Thomas Carlyle with
whom Emerson had struck up a friendship years before
during his first trip to Europe in 1833. Other sources
surmised that it might have been through the works of
Bishop Percy, another 19th century writer. Or perhaps it
was from Sharon Turner, the English historian whose work
*The History of the Anglo-Saxons from the Earliest Period
to the Norman Conquest* was documented to have been
read by Ralph Waldo Emerson (as mentioned earlier),

and was used by him as a basis for a few of his lectures in 1835. I was still trying to pinpoint an exact date of original exposure for one particular reason: In the book *The Vikings and the Victorians, Inventing the Old North in 19th Century Britain* written by Andrew Wawn in 2000, it states, "The most fundamental Viking-age belief was self reliance." In his own footnote to this concept, Wawn cites two sources, including George Dacent, another 19th century author that was read by Emerson. This was important to keep in mind.

In Barbara Packer's essay *Ralph Waldo Emerson*, which I had used for that 20-page January 2004 paper, she writes, "Emerson is warmly admiring of English skill and self-reliance" (It's interesting to note here that Barbara Packer uses a hyphen when spelling "self-reliance", and Andrew Wawn does not use the same punctuation tactic in his book.) Since a good number of Vikings that raided the British Isles decided to stay in order to put down roots, build farms, and raise families, a lasting Scandinavian community was created there as a result. There was a school of thought in the 19th century that the current at-the-time motivation for explorations of the Victorian British population perhaps had stemmed originally from this Viking influence. In my research, I was attempting to piece together why I thought Emerson was so intrigued with these stories, and I was striving to demonstrate this connection. This type of paper, though, was not what my supervisors had in mind.

They began to drop hints that I might not make it through the entire Ph.D. program if I did not begin to improve the written material that I was producing and submitting to them for evaluation. As mentioned before, my goal was to progress as time went on, and I felt discouraged when experiencing difficulty in finding a solution to this situation.

It was also during this time of heightened insecurity in late February 2004 that I decided to email Dr. Lawrence Buell once again, this time outlining my wish to travel to Cambridge, Massachusetts and read the original handwritten journals of Ralph Waldo Emerson to use as a primary source. In the email I detailed some of the most recent discoveries that I had uncovered in my research, including the above-mentioned sentence from Andrew Wawn's book *The Vikings and the Victorians* regarding the trait of self-reliance as a fundamental Viking Age value. Closing my eyes, I clicked "send" for the message to be delivered to his Harvard department email inbox, and hoped for the best. I had no expectations.

The month of March 2004 carried on in much the same way as February had done before it. I continued trying to find other scholars who had written about my topic, continued communicating with my advisors, and still strived to produce academic papers that would emit a "Well done!" response from them. I became so nervous developing one paper that I reworked it to the point where it was left simply in tatters. My confidence was dwindling. Finally, almost exactly a month after I had sent Dr. Buell that email, a momentous day occurred. During the afternoon on March 25, 2004, two apologies came my way, both via email. First I received an apology from my Danish supervisor regarding an unpleasant statement that had arrived in my inbox two days beforehand concerning my status as a Ph.D. student. The apology was appreciated; however, the statement had been quite negative.

Then, two hours after this upsetting email correspondence, I received an email from Dr. Lawrence Buell, apologizing for his delay in responding to my message a month before. He wrote that in his role as the Department Chair, he was able to authorize an appointment for me as an Associate to the English Department at Harvard for a six-month study duration any time that I was available to arrive within the next two years from the date of the sent email. The Associate status would allow me to have access to the Harvard library system and other resources at Harvard University to help me pursue my study of Ralph Waldo Emerson. This email (in contrast) was unbelievably kind. I was so thankful!

Feeling stunned after reading Dr. Buell's gracious email a few times, I had to sit down at my desk for a long while, simply absorbing this news. My mind went a little blank, as I fully realized what the news meant for my academic career. Finally, I called my stepfather in California with this newest development, knowing it was about 7:00 AM Pacific Standard Time. I didn't care. He picked up the phone and I told him what had happened. He listened carefully, then asked me to send him the email. He didn't believe me! He made me send him a copy of Dr. Buell's email so that he could read it himself. I sent him the email, then I elatedly replied to Dr. Buell's email with a resounding *yes* as my answer to his kind note. Hope came flooding back into my biological system. I was ready to go forward with renewed courage, and right at that moment, I started to make plans.

I knew it was imperative to stick to the schedule of the Ph.D. program to be certain that everything was in alignment, so I got out the calendar and reviewed the academic requirements. The first task was to contact the director of the graduate program at Roskilde in order to receive her official approval, which happened pretty quickly. I then arranged for my 6-month appointment to study at Harvard to begin in August 2004.

I also knew that it was still necessary to stay in Denmark until June 2004 and finish out the semester satisfactorily as a Ph.D. student, so I began planning carefully for that as well. Nonetheless, the fact that my research had been officially recognized as "out of the ordinary" by an outside academic source was such a feeling of joy that it made the experience of the previous few weeks much more bearable. I was absolutely elated! I began to look forward towards the new adventure, and this gave me the energy and strength that I needed to continue planning.

In early April 2004, I sent both a writing and research sample to Dr. Buell and the Harvard English department coordinator at the time, Ms. Anna McDonald, clarifying the latest aspect of the topic that I had been working on. At the same time, I also sent a copy of my resume for their records. Then, I set about planning for the three months that remained in the academic year at Roskilde University.

It became increasingly clear to me that there existed a necessity to find my own sources of assistance, improve on my own, and then turn in an "improved style" for my next submitted paper. My own version of self-reliance, so to speak. I opted to adapt a "When in Rome" attitude about the entire thing and consequently identify some additional sources of information. This was frustrating in and of itself since I realized it might truly make a difference to see more scholarly work on the subject that I was researching, even without the Scandinavian component. So I decided to ask another American scholar on Emerson for help since neither of my supervisors, as stated earlier, were experts on Ralph Waldo Emerson.

A year previously, I had read about Professor Ann Woodlief at Virginia Commonwealth University, and after seeing a study guide of hers posted online for her classes, I sent her an email asking for her help. Professor Woodlief kindly answered my email, and was very friendly and willing to help in any way that she could, which I greatly appreciated. We exchanged a few emails in mid-April 2004, and she sent me links to online pages so that I could see that most of the academic papers I was reading were quite similar in terms of writing style and research level to my own. Only one example was a much more dense style of writing and research than I had previously seen, fully-packed with various references in a shorter amount of space and sentences, though this may have been a post-doc research paper. Regardless, I was still relieved to see anything that was even close in terms of Ph.D. style and content covering the topic of Ralph Waldo Emerson that was similar to the papers that I had been submitting. I now had something on which to compare to my own writing in order to reach that vague level I had been told was necessary for me to reach, even after my invitation to continue my research short-term at Harvard University.

I wrote a final paper for the end of that semester, which admittedly was not my best work since at that point I felt perhaps the writing would still not meet their standards. Fortunately, my supervisors decided that my submitted paper was passable (but still not perfectly passable). In an email, it was affirmed that my writing style was of acceptable academic level. Nevertheless, the feeling was that the content in the paper still did not contain a proper analysis of Emerson's writings. All of my attempts to explain to my supervisors that I could not find multiple resources was futile; they felt that I simply wasn't trying hard enough and did not know how to properly conduct scholarly research. What I did not find out until I actually arrived at Harvard was that scholarly analysis comparing and contrasting contemporary scholars' published research, opinions, and ideas regarding Ralph Waldo Emerson and his use of Nordic Mythology which was lacking from my thus far submitted academic papers was lacking for a reason: Published works in contemporary scholarship of this topic simply had not been conducted before on a wide, or even narrow, scale. I could not find these studies because they were, quite literally, not available. They hadn't been done.

As the semester at Roskilde came to an end, I checked the tasks off my list that still needed to be completed in order to leave Denmark and move to Cambridge, Massachusetts. It seemed so long ago that I had gone through a similar process to leave Germany to move to Denmark, and yet it had only been a few years. The same procedure as when I moved from Portland, Oregon to Tübingen, Germany, as well, repeated itself for what was written on the list: complete the academic requirements for the semester, finish the professional obligations, return the documents to their proper places, pack up my things in boxes, clean the room, hand over the keys, and leave things wrapped up and tidy. It was time to continue the Ralph Waldo Emerson research journey, this time in the place where he was born, grew up, lived his life and made his mark in the world: Massachusetts, USA.

"Emerson is warmly admiring of English skill and self-reliance."

-Barbara Packer, *Ralph Waldo Emerson*

Harvard University, Cambridge

and

The Old Manse, Concord

Massachusetts

2004

After freshly arriving in Cambridge, Massachusetts, in early August 2004, I met with Dr. Lawrence Buell in his office on August 10 (the administrators from Harvard had offered me a J-1 visa assuming I was a Danish student; this made my friends smile, regarding my "reverse exchange student," status, i.e., an American student studying at a Danish university traveling to study for six months abroad as an exchange student to the USA. This was a highly unusual situation.)

Dr. Buell sat me in his office and quietly explained that the reason I had been invited to Harvard was because I was one of very few people studying a topic similar to mine. This was also the exact reason that I couldn't find any scholarly work on it to perform the contemporary critical analysis that my supervisors insisted that I do. I wasn't a bad scholar. I had simply experienced difficulty finding studies to use in my papers because there were very few studies on this topic to be found. Mine was a pioneering project. There weren't many scholars who had performed extensive research on this angle, whether in their own study or as editors to Emerson's lectures, writings, and journals. This information was both a surprise to me and also - an enormous feeling of relief! I knew that Dr. Phillip L. Nicoloff had conducted a study and written a book covering Emerson's volume of English Traits in 1961, but his analysis covered a slightly different focus than my proposed study. It also meant realizing that I had to make this study operate as a foundation for future scholars. Taking in this information, I decided to contact a few local specialists, and then to begin reading the available handwritten journals of Ralph Waldo Emerson located in Houghton Library in chronological order. Examining those journals in that calm historic library turned out to be some of my most contented moments spent at Harvard, which I did not anticipate. I was happy to be there.

During my first few months in Cambridge, I was also looking for a source of funding, as my appointment at Harvard was official, but unpaid. I wrote to the American-Scandinavian House and Foundation in New York, asking what was available in terms of grants and scholarships, and the reply I received stated that their organization did not have a scholarship that would pertain to my situation at Harvard; therefore I should instead apply to the Visiting Scholars Program at the American Academy of Arts & Sciences located in Massachusetts, which might offer more possibilities. The woman who communicated with me from this second institution, Alexandra Oleson, was quite nice and helpful, and explained the criteria in which most of the recipients' topics were categorized, yet the topic of my research did not fit into any of those categories.

She encouraged me to apply anyway, which I did. However, I was not awarded a grant or scholarship from them.

Still taking into account my financial situation, I asked the English department at Harvard for permission to stay for an entire year instead of six months, since I had to work in order to fund my stay. They very graciously allowed me to do this, so I wrote to Roskilde to ask their permission as well, and they were also willing to comply with this request. At the end of the year (I was told), I needed to send a fifty-page paper to my supervisors at Roskilde to be evaluated. That was fine by me, so I agreed. With this understanding in place, I was set, academically at least, to stay a full year in Massachusetts to continue researching my topic. I felt nearly certain I would be able to produce a paper that would satisfy my supervisors by that point in time.

This end-of-year paper is included at the back of this book. It is in raw form, and edited only in format to fit the sizing parameters of the book. Much of the information included in the paper are the details of evidence that I discovered while researching during this academic year at Harvard, and the connections between all of the evidence that I had found.

As mentioned before, one of my primary goals was to speak to local scholars themselves, at Harvard and at certain places in Concord, Massachusetts, such as the Concord Free Public Library, the Ralph Waldo Emerson House, the Concord Museum, and at the historical house, the Old Manse. I decided to talk to the people I could locate in Cambridge first. The initial scholar I met with was Christopher Irmscher, whom I was told I should contact. He was a very nice man and felt that my topic of study was a good one, and he suggested a few avenues to follow up with in my research, for which I was entirely grateful. A short time after our meeting, I contacted several other scholars including Dr. Phillip L. Nicoloff, Dr. Robert Burkholder, and I also sent a letter to Margaret (Bay) Bancroft, who is a direct descendant of Ralph Waldo Emerson. I received very gracious replies from both Dr. Nicoloff and Margaret Bancroft, which I absolutely appreciated. Dr. Burkholder did not respond.

I then made an appointment at Houghton Library to be introduced as a visitor to their collections system. Once I was familiar with signing in for manuscripts and reading them on-site, it became more comfortable and routine to go there several times a week. Much of my time was then spent reading the handwritten journals of Ralph Waldo Emerson looking for clues, side notes, or drawings that he might have made on the pages (marginalia) that can be more impactful when viewing them in their original form. I literally started with the very first journal, and began to read; fortunately I found the evidence that I was looking for almost immediately, which was incredibly encouraging! One was a poem that Emerson had written at age seventeen, the other was a fanciful story with a character named Uilsa, also including the name Odin (the head deity in Northern Mythology) and indicating that he (Odin) was from the north. I was inspired and overjoyed!

This discovery of the poem and the fictional short story in Ralph Waldo Emerson's earliest journals meant that my theories had been correct all along. As mentioned before, I had discovered some notes in his journals regarding his thoughts on Sharon Turner's writings, so any idea of the self-reliant trait of the Vikings was something that he was familiar with while he was a student at Harvard. Finding these creative writings in his earliest journals meant something more; that Emerson appreciated the Scandinavian stories enough to use them to create original fictitious work of his own. To double-check, I wrote a few emails to Dr. Buell to make certain that it was an original poem of Emerson's in his journals and not something that he copied from somewhere else; Dr. Buell's quick reply assured me that it was an original creation of Emerson's. Up until that point, my main focus had been to prove Emerson had indeed known about the Scandinavian Vikings long before he had written any of his professional lectures or essays. This had now not only been proven, but a new facet had also surprisingly been added.

As the academic year went on, I continued to return to the Houghton Library to read the original journals of Ralph Waldo Emerson in chronological order. On a daily basis, though, I still carried with me two standout emotions; elation at being at Harvard University and finding all of these fantastic new pieces of evidence while conducting my research, and also feeling an increasing amount of disconnect from my supervisors in Denmark. No matter how many little nuggets of verification and insight I discovered bit-by-bit, I was still a little worried that my research would not be enough to satisfy my Danish supervisors' idea of what would be acceptable to them as a Ph.D. level of writing. So I decided to expand my research even more, and looked at as much history surrounding the Viking trading routes as possible, to add to my reasons of why Emerson would be fascinated by them. I researched the Danes who went west and invaded England several times; the Norwegians who went west and traveled to Scotland, Ireland (and founded the Irish cities of Dublin and Cork), Iceland, Greenland, and Newfoundland in Canada; and the Swedes who headed towards the east, to the Baltic countries, Russia and Constantinople, the Caspian Sea, and the Byzantine Empire. Much of what I found in this regard is widely available public knowledge; currently there are many maps produced depicting the trade routes of the Vikings, including routes heading south around the coast of Spain. This information all came together well to fill in several components that added to the growing body of research and documentation that I was compiling, and it made for a better study and more complete collection of evidentiary support.

It was still important to me to find out when Emerson was first exposed to the history and the stories of the Scandinavian Vikings in relation to when he formulated his own perception of the concept of self-reliance. As Ann Woodlief had written to me in an email back in April 2004, various scholars have remarked that 'Self-Reliance' was a basis for nearly everything that Emerson wrote. If the Viking Age belief was self-reliance (as was noted by Andrew Wawn), and consequently a British/English trait was also self-reliance (as noted in Barbara Packer's essay), then that may have also been the then identified source of self-reliance that helped shape the entire philosophical backbone which infiltrated all of Emerson's works. What was also interesting to me, which I had already explored a bit in Denmark, were the qualities that went along with the self-reliant trait of the

Vikings that may have also been attractive to Ralph Waldo Emerson. There are some very clear codes of conduct that were detailed in *Havamal*, located within the *Poetic Edda*, which seem to show up in one way or another in Emerson's sermons, lectures, writings and teachings. Nevertheless, it is the trait of self-reliance that continued to stand out again and again in these printed works.

Consequently, I then went through a process trying to decide how to figure out how far back the exposure of the Nordic sources just might have been. Emerson's journals that are kept at Harvard only begin in 1819, so in order to find earlier writings I would need to implement some form of ingenuity. Therefore, I spoke with David Wood, Curator for the Concord Museum, requesting to see the collection of books from Emerson's study, which had been transferred to the Concord Museum from the Emerson house, conveniently located just down the street. Mr. Wood mentioned that some of the books had been moved around from the house to the museum and even to Harvard library collections, and that I should be aware of this. More often than not, he said, the book collection lists were fairly accurate for each location. Leslie Wilson, Curator of the Special Collections at the Concord Free Public Library at the time, expressed something similar when I spoke to her regarding this topic. She was a longtime resident of Concord, and had lots of enthusiasm concerning the collections that they had available in the archives of the Concord Free Library. After speaking with these two experts and researching various places, I realized that the book collection that I most needed to examine was at the Old Manse, where Ralph Waldo Emerson spent intervals of time during his childhood. If I could match even a portion of the Old Manse books to the topic at hand, and especially the dates of the publications of those books and periodicals, then I could prove that Emerson probably knew about Scandinavian Vikings and their self-reliant traits all the way back to when he was a child. I asked Dr. Buell to please write a letter on my behalf requesting permission from the Trustees of Reservations, the organization that runs many of the historical houses in Massachusetts including the Old Manse, for approval to spend a few months during the summer researching this collection of books at the Old Manse. Thankfully, that request was granted; the letter was written by him to the Trustees, and the Trustees sent me a dated letter with permission. So, beginning in the early summer of 2005, I made many trips to the Old Manse to view their collection of books, and to see what was there. John Daly, the Assistant Site Manager filling in for the Site Manager who was on leave, greeted me when I first arrived at the front door.

John turned out to be a delightful person and very enthusiastic for the project, and I was fortunate to have him to oversee the sifting through the materials on site looking for books that fit into a certain publication time frame that might have anything to do with Scandinavia or the Vikings. He and some of the volunteers explained to me that at a historical site such as the Old Manse, many volunteers would often work simultaneously on a list of books attempting to categorize what exactly was in the collections. Since the group was precisely that (volunteers), there were times that some helpers would leave, and a new group would start the list of books all over again for a "new improved list", thereby compiling several concurrent lists of books that had begun at various dates and years. With this information, the lists of books provided to me were helpful (there were a few thousand volumes of books at the time), but I was encouraged to look through as many of the actual books on site within the house and in the annex as possible, since some volumes of books in the house might differ from what was written on the list.

Therefore, during that summer of 2005, I systematically started going through the books in the house, with white cotton gloves on. I must have looked in nearly every book in the house, in the hallway, and the rooms of the second floor of the Old Manse. The real treasures, however, were the books that were kept in the boxes and on the shelves in the second story of the annex of the house (these books have since been moved to an outside facility). Climbing up into that space with multiple book lists in my hand for guidance, I looked through bookshelf after bookshelf and box after box, searching for publications with specific date ranges that would have been in the family collection at the time that Ralph Waldo Emerson was a young child. I found so many sources of evidence that I could barely stop myself from smiling! As previously documented by the footnotes in hardcover versions of Ralph Waldo Emerson's journals (the details of the volume are located in my Author's Note in the front of this book), Emerson was reading the Edinburgh Review publications during his time as a student at Harvard. Many issues of the Edinburgh Review published with comparable and earlier dates were included in the literary collections I found at the Old Manse. There were also multiple volumes of the Encyclopaedia Britannica there as well, which offered additional physical clues with evidence of written passages having been read or marked as significant. For example, in one of the reference books, a corner of the page was turned down (earmarked) clearly indicating that someone thought it important enough to mark it separately (either show to another person, or return to read it later). To showcase an additional example, a leaf found on the page of Saxony and Scandinavia in an Encyclopaedia Britannica had been there for so long that an imprint of the leaf was now permanently stained on the page. A photocopy of this page is in the back of this book. The image is quite remarkable.

Another publication I found within the collection that proved to be a keystone piece of evidence was Andrew Swinton's book *Travels into Norway, Denmark, and Russia, in the Years 1788, 1789, 1790, and 1791*. This book is significant because it is included in an 1822 catalogue of books marked as 'a set of 8 Swinton's Travels' belonging to William Emerson (Ralph Waldo's father) which was scheduled to be sold at public auction on August 27th at the Theological Library in Massachusetts, therefore we know that this book belonged to William Emerson. His bookplate also happens to be affixed to the inside cover. Both a photocopy of the book plate and one of the cover of Swinton's Travels are also included in the back of this book. The list of William Emerson's books slated for sale at the 1822 auction can be found in the Library at Harvard University.

Some of the books I looked through had actual handwriting on the cover or inside the book. One of these books, *The History of England, From the Invasion of Julius Caesar to the Revolution in MDCLXXXVIII in Six Volumes, Volume 1*, by David Hume, proved to be yet another keystone in the connection between Ralph Waldo Emerson and his early knowledge of the Scandinavians. On one of the inside pages, there is a handwritten list of historical events, beginning with "orig[inal] Inhab[itants]- II Cesar. [sic]." This list depicts first the Romans, then the Saxons, followed by the native kings (including Alfred the Great), and the Danish Kings as well. These events on the list occurred in Britain both during and before the Viking Age. This chart was an incredible find, not only because of the handwritten dates of the chart, but also because it meant that someone wanted to preserve the historical timeline as a keepsake for personal or professional use. The chart's dates and names (a photocopy of it is included at the back of this book) are not written in a recognizable handwriting (although - wouldn't it be fun if an expert reading this book could identify who had written down that chart?). After viewing this chart, I also fully acknowledged that many of the sources that were available for reading at the Old Manse regarding the ancient Scandinavians also described their possible origins. These various writings, then, took 'the question' much farther back than the Viking Age.

All of the sudden I understood that I would be researching earlier in history than I had anticipated, because the questions had expanded. It was no longer enough to wonder how young Ralph Waldo Emerson was when he first learned about the self-reliant traits of the Scandinavian Vikings. It became something even more profound: From where did the Scandinavians themselves originate? There were so many published resources at the Old Manse with conflicting possibilities debating this question that I devoted approximately ten pages of my year-end submitted paper for my Roskilde supervisors to this very topic. It was absolutely fascinating to consider that 19th century and earlier writers, authors, and various sources had speculated where the Scandinavians themselves may have migrated from to become the first Scandinavians. Celts, Goths, Scythians, Asians and Gauls were some of the possibilities that I found these writers were contemplating in the available materials on the shelves of the Old Manse. Since I knew I wanted to include as much relevant material as I could, I made photocopies of nearly everything that I found at the Old Manse pertaining to this topic. I've included the full six-page handwritten list that I compiled of the books, manuscripts, and periodicals that I used in this study, with the intent of providing resource information for future scholars.

That amazing investigative summer in 2005 helped me to have a deep appreciation and respect for the Old Manse, and kept me coming back as a volunteer for several years after this initial research expedition. This included a time a few years later in the summer in 2008 when we put together a volunteer team to catalog all of the written materials on site and transport those rare volumes to a temperature-controlled facility to be preserved for future use. Sorting through all of that evidence first-hand was an unforgettable experience, and one that was absolutely sublime in its own right.

After I felt that I had looked through as many books as possible and had amassed enough evidence from the abundance of original sources at the Old Manse, the moment of truth had arrived. It was time to assemble all of the primary resources that I had collected from the original journals and other sources at the Harvard libraries, books at the Concord Museum, and of course the multitude of old published material at the Old Manse, to document all of these incredible resources as containing the evidence that detailed the self-reliant Scandinavian Vikings stories, both historical events and myths alike. The written opinions of contemporary-at-the-time authors (those in the 19th century) regarding the Norse activities brought all of these virtues and self-reliant ideals to light, and provided a foundation for Emerson to feasibly form his own definition of self-reliance while he was still young. I had discovered plenty of original sources while conducting my research to establish that these proofs of evidence indeed still existed in tangible form, and continued to be available for other researchers to study going forward.

Therefore, I gathered all of my evidence up, and wrote a fifty-one page paper to fulfill the fifty-page requirement for the program supervisors in Denmark, including references specifying all of the evidence that I had collected. When finished, I sent a copy of this paper electronically via my Harvard email account multiple times from several different computer terminals to ensure that it would get to Denmark safely. Once the verification came through that the paper had been received, my two supervisors took a few weeks to evaluate the work.

Unfortunately, they did not react favorably to my paper. A formal review was then written up and sent to me. The heading paragraph on the top acknowledged that I had conclusively proven my query topic with facts: "We acknowledge that you have now answered the subheading 'Proof that R.W. Emerson...' in the affirmative," It begins, "and that you have dug out sources, notably from 'Old Manse' as evidence. We also acknowledge that your sources and investigations are adequate in proving that point. Finally, it is clear that you have made quite some effort in producing these pages." I felt hopeful after reading the first sentences of the review.

Then, the evaluation turned rather negative. My Danish supervisors reviewed this fifty-one page paper, with original resources as evidence for the research, and decided that it was not a passable piece of written work. I was truly confused by this outcome, for several reasons; I knew that the research findings were solid, and I also felt dismayed because my supervisors had informed me that my writing style was of passable Ph.D. level a year before when I left Denmark. It didn't make sense to me.

Regardless, upon inquiry, I was informed as per the regulations of Roskilde University at that time that I would be allowed some additional months after receiving this review in which I could update, make changes, and generally revise the fifty-one pages to an improved degree. I absorbed this news, looked at the calendar, and calculated how long I had in order to send them an updated document.

In the middle of November 2005, I received an email from Karen Sonne Jakobsen, the head of the department, letting me know that a revision had been received and evaluated on a second formal review of my paper. This "second version" had also been rejected, and Ms. Jakobsen wrote that she was very sorry but that the recommendation to terminate my participation from the program was now in place. There was, however, one minor detail to this story. I had not sent a revision of my paper. They had read the exact same version of the original paper twice, and evaluated it twice, without realizing it. Needless to say, this entire turn of events was rather upsetting. I wrote to Karen Sonne Jacobsen and pointed out this error, which she then investigated and later verified. After a few more back-and-forth emails and a subsequent search for alternate advisors had been conducted, in April 2006 I was offered the opportunity of finding an academic supervisor of my choosing, and it was suggested that I ask various scholars in Massachusetts to find myself a suitable advisor.

I, of course, immediately asked Dr. Lawrence Buell if he would be available to continue to supervise my continued research. He said his time was already overextended, but that he had someone in mind. Dr. Buell then contacted Dr. Ronald A. Bosco from the University of Albany, State University of New York, to see if he would be willing to take over as supervisor for this project, and fortunately for me, he agreed. Dr. Bosco and I worked very well together in Massachusetts for the next year, and in March 2007, I withdrew from the Rosklide University program, electing instead to continue my Ralph Waldo Emerson research in the United States.

(Author's collection, Concord Edition)

"To believe your own thought, to believe that what is true for you in your private heart is true for all men - that is genius."

-Ralph Waldo Emerson, *Self-Reliance*

Epilogue

2006 - Present Day

There is more of this story to be told after that spring of 2006, including the adventure of finding even more astounding items while looking through additional boxes in the Old Manse as a volunteer during the following three years. In late summer of 2008, A team of experts and volunteers gathered together, and we went through nearly every item on the shelves and in cardboard containers within the house (not including the basement). This volunteer team was initiated by Dr. Tom Beardsley, who held the position as the Old Manse Site Manager at the time. Our volunteer crew cleaned, sorted, and categorized the boxes in the attic of the Old Manse, in a manner which had not been conducted before this effort to that extent. Once it was all organized, we moved most of the rare books and one-of-a-kind items from the Old Manse to both the Concord Free Library and to the (at the time) newly-opened state-of-the-art climate-controlled facility in Sharon, Massachusetts, for preservation and safe-keeping of the items. This experience was as unique as some of the books that we transferred, and the feeling of protecting and preserving history for the sake of posterity was simply euphoric. There are no other words.

Among the multiple items that we discovered among the collection included a copy of the original signed house deeds for the Old Manse from the late

1800s, a letter from Thomas Carlyle still inside the stamped envelope, and an original publication of *The Dial*. I remember finding both the letter from Thomas Carlyle with the over-a-century old postage stamp still affixed, and the 1842 volume of *The Dial*; I literally to sit down in a chair with weak knees after I realized what exactly it was that I held in my hand! We also found some handwritten papers that seemed to be possible loose pages from a 19th century diary, at which point we called in an expert, Dr. Robert A. Gross from the University of Connecticut, to verify the pages. Then, our volunteer group grew larger. I may document these experiences of cleaning, organizing, and cataloging all of those items during that summer of 2008 in a later book. It was nothing short of extraordinary.

For many years, it was my aim to finish my Ph.D. degree at a later time at a university in the United States. I applied to and was accepted into a pre-Ph.D. study program at Northeastern University within a short time of submitting my application during the summer of 2007. I had just begun a new full-time job while enrolled in that program that required unforeseen overtime, and could not devote the time and energy needed to complete the program, which was extremely frustrating. Two years later I moved back to Northern California, to be near my family, and later moved to San Diego where I was an

English as a Foreign Language instructor for several
years. I applied twice to a Ph.D. program in Southern
California, with no success. In-between these years I
attended multiple Modern Language Association
conferences, and was a participant in a writing seminar
held in San Francisco, meeting with representatives and
literary agents from publishing houses during all of these
conventions. My topic, however, was so unique that I
found myself having the same conversation over and
over again - one that involved the recognition that my
research did not fall into a specific category and therefore
it would be difficult to identify a target audience. One
agent rejected the work with the reasoning that the topic
was "far enough afield" from other Emerson research
topics to be accepted by his publishing house. This was
indeed disappointing news after three months of email
communication with him following an in-person meeting
at an MLA conference.

The Emerson scholars that I met during my years
as a Ph.D. candidate and afterwards understood the
importance of the research that I had conducted, and I
was encouraged multiple times by these experts not to
give up and to continue to apply to programs and attend
as many conferences, conventions, and seminars as I
could. They collectively advised that no matter what the
situation, I should stay optimistic, and to keep safe all of

the physical evidence that I had collected during my years of study. I was assured that it was important to maintain a positive attitude, and to trust that one day I would be able to publish my findings and continue my research on the journals and works of Ralph Waldo Emerson. That day has arrived, and I am overjoyed.

-Elizabeth S. Scofield

(Author's Note: This is one of the final versions of the 2002 proposal submitted. Some citation and formatting errors are noticeable in this version, however I have chosen to include them as part of the original).

Original Proposal:
Scandinavian Influences in
Emerson's Writings for the
Lecture Series in England
2002

Title: The Scandinavian Influences in Emerson's Writings for the Lecture Series in England, 1847-1848, and for his Manuscript "English Traits", Published 1856.

To the Director of the Department of Department of Languages and Culture:

I wish to apply to be a Research Degree student in the Department of History and Social Theory at Roskilde University. I am interested in studying specifically at Roskilde because of the offered research degree in "European Cultural Studies". To quote from the Roskilde University website, I believe this is a logical continuation of my M.A. degree, and would allow me to persist in what I am most passionate about, mainly the research and study of culture and history, and communication. I propose to write a Research Degree thesis with the title of: **The Scandinavian Influences in Emerson's Writings for the Lecture Series in England, 1847-1848, and for the Manuscript "English Traits", Published 1856**. This project would also fit the "Modernisation of Consciousness in Culture and Literature" theme in the Department of Languages and Culture because of the aspect of Emerson, his ideals and influence/effectiveness towards changing the rush of industry in the 19th century American society Emerson was a lecturer, writer, and philosopher in the 19th century, well-known in his time and still popular today. He was a key participant of a group of writers and later reformers called the Transcendentalists that surged onto the literary and social American scene between the 1830's and 1850's, with the main interest of attempting to slow down the entire industrial revolution, by (re)introducing the idea of mankind connecting to nature in a more direct way than had been customary previously to this time in the United States. In the years 1847-1848, Emerson traveled to England and gave a series of lectures there over the course of six months; interestingly enough, the essays entitled "English Traits" were not published until 1856. In many of these essays, he remarks that the strength of the English character comes from the Danes. To quote from the introduction of The Journals of Ralph Waldo Emerson, volume X, from 1847-1848 "Passages from *Northern Antiquities* and *The Younger Edda* show an interest in Scandinavian myth and legend that anticipates the early chapters of *English Traits;* reading the *Edda* in 1847 and later the *Heimskringla*, a history of Norse kings, that he brought back from England in 1848." Emerson was also a great admirer of Swedenborg, and managed to offend some members of his British audience when he presented the lecture "Swedenborg" in Manchester and Liverpool, to the point that some civilians, who were a cult organisation called 'Swedenborgians" attempted to get the rest of his lectures cancelled.

Background Of Emerson

Ralph Waldo Emerson was a philosopher, lecturer and literary mover in the United States during the 19th century. Transcendentalism began as a reform movement against the Unitarian church, which was the predominant religion in the early 19th century in New England, and in itself, developed out of a branch of Liberal Christianity in the 1740's. Transcendentalism has been deemed not to be a religion precisely, but a type of philosophy, that considers each person to have the ability to receive the divinity of God individually, without the need of a minister to intervene. Transcendentalism also incorporates the doctrine of self-fulfilment by looking at nature, appreciating it, and marvelling at it. With this mentality, the Transcendentalists gained ground. Emerson was at the forefront of this new reflection era, from 1820 until 1860—he stood out as the commanding voice of the movement. Other self-called Transcendentalists were Margaret Fuller, Walt Whitman, Henry David Thoreau, and Bronson Alcott just to name a few. Soon they were also trying to create a new body of American literature, with essays, novels, poetry and other works unique and uninfluenced by Europe, but many of the Transcendentalists also cried out for social reform, including improvements in the educational system, women's rights and especially relating to Emerson, anti-slavery. The Dial, a periodical put out by the Transcendentalist circle between the years 1840-1844, expressed and spread the ideas, thoughts and writings of the Transcendentalist movements. Margaret Fuller was the editor for the first two years, And Emerson for the latter two. Transcendentalists spread their ideas not only through publication, but through lecturing as well. Emerson became well-known for his lecturing style and presence, and became increasingly in demand.

Emerson's career was followed by Alexander Ireland, managing editor of the Manchester Examiner newspaper. Ireland was interested in the then-active movement in England and Scotland for the betterment of the working class people, by raising their awareness of things intellectual, cultural and educational. Lectures were a crucial aspect of part of this reform, it was felt at the time. Ireland had heard about Emerson personally from Margaret Fuller, another Transcendentalist, on her trip to England in 1846. Ireland wrote to Emerson on November 4, 1846, and invited him to do the series of lectures. Emerson borrowed the book of Northern Antiquities: Or, A Description of the Manners, Customs, Religion and Laws of the Ancient Danes —a version translated in London by Bishop Thomas Percy in 1770-- from the Harvard College Library on July 26, 1847. That same month, he accepted Alexander Ireland's invitation to do the series of lectures all over England and Scotland. Emerson left Boston on October 5, 1847, and arrived in Liverpool in October 22nd of the same year.

Scandinavian Influence in 19th Century England

A revival of interest in the old Scandinavian legends and stories came about in Europe in the late 19th century, specifically by Wagner, who used the Edda and Sagas as part of the base for the Ring

Operas—the Ring cycle was finished in 1874. In
Britain, William Scott cultivated an interest in
Scottish Norse history, and his novel "The Pirate"
was published in 1822. Various members of the
pre-Raphaelite movement, including William Morris,
were intrigued by Scandinavian Romanticism;
Morris even honed his passion for medieval
Scandinavia after studying at Oxford by learning
Old Icelandic and translating several of the sagas,
journeying to Iceland in 1871 and 1873. During the
nineteenth century, Anglo-Saxon and Old Norse
were made available as university subjects. English
historians during the early part of the 19th century
mostly thought of the Scandinavians as warriors,
and not as having made a significant contribution to
their history. To quote Samuel Laing, who
translated The Younger Edda in London in 1844,
"These Northmen have not merely been the
forefathers of the people, but of the institutions and
character of the nation, to an extent not sufficiently
considered by our historians" (p A2) However, that
notion began to change as the century wore on.

In Old Icelandic, "vik" meant bay, or creek, or it may
have been used to describe anyone from a region
in Oslofjord, southern Norway. The Old Icelandic

verb "vikya" meant to turn aside, and the Icelandic Sagas use the term "vikingr" to indicate a warrior or pirate, and "Viking" meant an expedition. In the raids on the United Kingdom, different Vikings went to different locations, and most were identified simply as Danes, even though they were certainly Swedes, Norwegians and Danish combined. They settled and mixed with the Anglo-Saxons of England, and, even though they were met with some resistance and scorn for invading, were soon blended with the people and incorporated into the lifestyle. Whereas many Scandinavian forays were made on English territory during the late eighth and early ninth centuries, England didn't fall under the rule of Denmark until the middle of the tenth century; the invasion lasted for 250 years. Hence, the sagas were a good indication of the beliefs and values of the Scandinavian people who merged into the British population during this time.

The Books on Scandinavia that Emerson Absorbed

The stories of the Younger Edda and the Heimsrkingla were the Norse Mythology tales read by Emerson. Snorre (sometimes spelled Snorri, or Snorro) Sturluson (or Sturleson) was the person who originally wrote down the Younger (Prose) Edda, also known as the Snorre Edda. Born in Iceland in 1178, and married in to a wealthy and prominent family when he was in his twenties, He then became quite powerful and prominent, and had battles joined with his brothers against other powers, as well as against the brothers themselves. He then went to Norway for many years, and left in 1239 at the wishes of King Hakon, who was later murdered by the united front of several Icelandic chiefs. Snorre was Iceland's most distinctive and illustrious skald and sagaman. His Heimskringla is an elaborate telling of history of the Kings of Norway, and an English translation was published by Samuel Laing in 1844 as mentioned above, which was read by Emerson. The Younger Edda was translated into English and published by Bishop Percy, in his edition of Paul Henri Mallet's Northern Antiquities: Or, A Description of the Manners, Customs, Religion and Laws of the Ancient Danes...With a Translation of the Edda (Mallet's version itself published in French in the 1756).

Emerson continued to be influenced and fascinated by the Norse mythology even after his return from

England, according to his journals. He presented the idea of the Vikings/Danes/Northmen as the backbone to the English character in writing, in the book "English Traits" published in 1856, with many passages about these Danish qualities specifically in the essays "Race", "Ability" "Truth" "Character" and "Aristocracy". He incorporated the myths, characters and ideas into later lectures, including "Instinct and Inspiration", and two lectures from the series, "Conduct of Life", published in 1860. He wrote passages of the Heimskrigla into his journals, with admiration. He shared his interest in the Heimskringla with friends Bronson Alcott and Thomas Carlyle, even reading passages to Alcott aloud. Several of the texts are still found in the Emerson library, Including the Heimskringla, as he states in his journals, "I bring home the Heimskringla, or seakings of Norway, translated by Samuel Laing, 1844" (page 336). The Ecclesiastical History of England, Also the Anglo-Saxon Chronicle, written by Beda Venerabilis, edited by J.A. Giles (London, 1847), can also be found there, as well as Northern Mythology, Comprising the Principle Popular of Traditions and Superstitions of Scandinavia, North Germany, and the Netherlands, written by Benjamin Thorpe in 3 volumes. (London,

1851-1852). Emerson had volumes II and III. He also read The Prose or Younger Edda commonly ascribed to Snorri Sturluson, translated from Old Norse by George Webbe Dasent, B.A. Stockholm and London 1842. Emerson refers to several of these volumes in his journals.

Manuscripts Reveal Influences

Emerson said, "The presence of divine spirit in both nature and the human soul made a direct understanding of God and an openness to the natural world avenues to self-understanding as well to the perception of broader truth and morality. A human intuition is all that is needed to sense divinity in both self, other people and nature, uniting all." Throughout Emerson's popularity, a less rational, more intuitive, more sensory-based manner of thought became more prominent. From the previously mentioned manuscripts, each book has references in the prefaces and introductions by the original editors that describe something about the beliefs of the Danes that reflect Transcendentalist views, as well the importance of the Danish stock. Several passages expose this: From Laing, "Is not the real inward sentiment in the mind of man, with regard to the Divinity, the same, precisely the same, whatever the mode of expressing it?" (p 73) He continues with, "The principles, spirit, and forms of legislation through which they work in our social union, are the legitimate offspring of the Things of the Northmen, not of the Wittenagemoth of the Anglo-Saxons—of the independent Norse Viking, not of the abject Saxon Monk" (p 107). From Thorpe, "Man's ambition is two-fold: he will not only live in the minds of prosperity; he will also have lived in ages long gone by; he looks not only forwards, but backwards also; and no people on earth is indifferent to the fancied honour of being able to trace its origin to the gods, and of being ruled by an ancient race" (p 2). From Percy/Mallet: "The moment the soul, reflecting on its own operations recurs inwards, and detaches itself from exterior objects, the imagination loses energy, the passions their activity, the mind becomes severe, and requires ideas rather than sensations…the most affecting and most striking passages in the ancient northern poetry" (p 238). Interestingly enough, the manuscripts all critique each other's work as well; for example, the manuscript of Northern Antiquities refers throughout to Samuel Laing's translation of the Heimskringla.

Emerson said, "we walk on our own feet; we will work with our own hands; we will speak our own minds..." How could it be that such a well-respected man came to respect the Danish stock so much? I want to research this at Roskilde University because it is important to explore the Danish Spirit that Emerson was so intrigued with. Who were the Danes of the old legends, why were they so influential on him? And did he continue to admire those traits in people he met at the time? Danes pride themselves to be self-reliant, and independent. Danes appreciate active people who take the initiative and do things. How much of this is apparent in the sagas read by Emerson? How much of it was carried over by the authors and translators of the books that he read? The Danes believed in gods that were unique to the Nordic and northern European culture, rich in universal collective human drama and symbolism. I want to explore the various aspects of the ancient folklore, religious and non, and find out how much still existed in Emerson's time, as character traits. There is a growing interest among the Danes for their historic past and their culture, and there is little written on this connection with Emerson's writings in the 19th century.

Swedenborg

Emerson also held a deep appreciation of Emanuel Swedenborg, the Swedish philosopher. Swedenborg had a father that was a minister, like Emerson's, and his training was in mechanics, mathematics, and engineering. Later, he explored the human body and published 2 volumes with an intent of publishing eleven volumes in the second edition. His thought was if the body indeed housed the soul, then there must be some sort of magic to it. After this he turned to Christianity, and published loads of volumes including commentary on the Bible, explanations of the scriptures in a spiritual meaning and how they related to God, the spiritual history of humanity, and the individual spiritual pilgrimage. Emerson was influenced by much of Swedenborg's ideas and philosophies. He even wrote an entire essay entitled "Swedenborg" to be included in his lecture series "Representative Men". Emerson incorporated this Swedenborg lecture in his English Tour—and wound up offending Swedenborgians, because Emerson implied his displeasure that there were cult followers of the great Swedish man. He even wrote in his journal of 1847-1848 "what a misfortune is a Swedenborg

Church. It requires for the profitable reading of Swedenborg almost an equal understanding to his own" (p 162). His main borrowed issues were Swedenborg's concepts of the constant influx between the spiritual world and the natural world, with man in the middle, and the mysterious connection of individuals to other individuals. Most importantly, the idea that nature's highest value is to provide symbols of spiritual and moral truths; a person's education comes from deciphering the language of nature Transcendentalism is based on the idea that truth is innate in all of nature and that knowledge is intuitive rather than rational. According to Emerson, it is unnecessary for the Church to be the link between an individual and God. All of this is clearly evident in Emerson's writings and ideas.

One more aspect I would like to explore is what was happening politically at the time of Emerson's English lecture series, on both sides of the Atlantic, as well. When he traveled to and within England, it was right in the middle of the political dealings with Ireland and the Famine, and there is some mention of the situation in his journals. Was Emerson invited to deflect from the horrors of the 'Irish problem'?

Also, interestingly, in one lecture that he gave in the United States, he states that the American culture derives directly from European culture, and that it shouldn't; America should create its own—this was part of the Transcendental movement. They warned Americans that they, the Americans, were too materialistic and that they put too much emphasis on machines and technological values. However, once the British lecture series, entitled "English Traits", was published, Emerson criticises the Americans as being an inferior race, and culture. He wrote in his journals during his visit to England "If I stay here for long, I shall lose all my patriotism. And think that England has absorbed all excellences". (244)

The questions I want to answer are:

-Where did the interest in Scandinavia originate from?

-How did he first hear about the Norse mythologies, and why did he choose the books, and stories, that he did?

-What other admirations did he have for the Danes/ Northmen?

-Did he equate the ancient Norse tales with then present-day Scandinavians that he met?

-Were his ancestors of Scandinavian origin?

-What was precisely the Scandinavian contribution to the development of England? What was it about the Scandinavian character that meant that in some locations, for example the Danelaw, they blended and merged with local customs, and in others, for one, the Isle of Man, they continued to have a distinct culture?

-How much did he attribute Danish character to Americans? Was it through English descent, or directly from pre-Columbus Scandinavian settlements in America?

-How did he formulate his lectures to present to the English public?

-What happened to him after the lecture series, how did he use the material written, gathered, and saved, in future tours in lectures in the United States?

-How did it come to pass, that the book "English Traits" was not published until a full eight years after his return from England? Who edited his work, since much of the lectures presented in this book were as much about the English people themselves as including the descriptions of the speeches that he gave during the lecture tour? How did his views change as a result of that trip? And why did he not include all of the actual speeches that he did indeed use as his lectures there?

-How much impact did Emerson's personal fascination with the Norse mythological stories have on other writers, and other developments in literature?

METHODOLOGY/ WORK PLAN:

In a three--year time span, I believe it will take me:

-6 months to familiarize myself with the various identical works that Emerson read to become influenced about the Scandinavians; the very same translations of the Younger Edda and Heimskringla; these translations are available in Copenhagen. This time would include finding and discovering the various themes in the stories that mirror Emerson's philosophies, essays and lectures. I would also like to know who else was reading the stories at the time, and who else was affected by them (for example, Thomas Carlyle was also inspired by the Heimskringla and wrote an essay on the kings of Norway).

-4 months to find out about the Viking Spirit, stock, character—what was it that made Emerson admire them so much? What was it about the stories that made such an impact on him?

-3 months to document Emerson's life and works up until the point of the English Traits lecture series—his first jobs, what influenced him to become a lecturer, the process he went through, his first trip to Europe and how that influenced him and his writings.

-3 months to concentrate on the time frame of just before he accepted the invitation to do the British lecture series, July 1847—the same month he borrowed the Norse book from the Harvard Library— what convinced him to do so? How much of Northern Antiquities book was read and processed before the actual journey? What was happening politically on both sides of the Atlantic, what was happening in Emerson's life personally and professionally, what were the factors that convinced him to go and deliver the lecture series (He had declined previous offers to do so).

-4 months to document the journey there, years 1847-48—putting his affairs in order, booking the cabin on the ship, journey abroad, lecture series—preparing myself for his tour by reading journals written before and during his trip.

SEMESTER ABROAD: Journey to England to trace his series, and footsteps, document whom he met, where he went. Another option would be to travel to Boston, Massachusetts, to familiarize myself first-hand with time before and after the British trip taken.

-5 months to trace his life and works up until lecture series was published, eight years later—why so long to publish it? Political reasons? Or personal?

-3 months to edit.

Other Dissertations Concerning Emerson

There are a number of other dissertations that cover aspects of Emerson's writings, philosophy, and experience, none of them dealing exclusively with Scandinavian aspects. Titles of relevant dissertations I have found are:

Bense, Charles James "Emerson and Hawthorne as Cultural Reporters: A Revaluation of 'English Traits' and 'Our Old Home'" University of California, Davis, 1989, 394 pages --emphasizes that these two works have been critically undervalued as contributions to each author's lifetime achievements.

Bogart, Herbert "Ralph Waldo Emerson: Self and Society" New York University, 1963 433 pages—examines the essays of Society and Solitude, English Traits, and the Conduct of Life, and explores Emerson's belief in the possibility of cultural ideals of society affecting the egotistical self in a humanistic way.

Chang, Yao-Hsin, "Chinese Influence in Emerson, Thoreau, and Pound" Temple University, 1985, 334 pages—introduces Chinese and Confucian ideas, and shows where the ideas apply to the writings and teachings of Emerson, Thoreau and Pound.

Gouluboff, Benjamin Louis "The Confident Dream: American Travel Writing on England" 1820-1909.

University of Pennsylvania, 1986 227 pages–
contains analysis of abroad experiences of Cooper,
Emerson, Stowe, Irving, and others.

Meese, Elizabeth A. "Transcendental Vision: A
History of the Doctrine of Correspondence and its
Role in American Transcendentalism" Wayne State
University, 1972, 322 pages—broad study of the
role of Emerson in association with Swedenborg's
idea of correspondence.

Nicoloff, Philip L. "Emerson's Thoughts on English
Traits" Columbia University, 1959. Later published
as "Emerson on Race and History: an Examination
of English Traits" New York: Columbia University
Press, 1961. 315 pages—a comprehensive study
of English Traits.

Rowland, William Gordon, Jr. "Writers Against
Readers: English and American Romantic Writers
and the Nineteenth Century Reading Public"
University of Virginia, 1988, 414 pages—explores
the methods used by both American and English
writers to find ways to express their thoughts that
would satisfy not only themselves but the
publishers and readers, with an emphasis on
Ideology and Romanticism.

Smith, John Warren "Emerson's English Traits: A Critical and Annotated Study" University of Texas, 1957, 629 pages—a carefully construed introduction to the work, and compares it to similar writings of other authors. Includes a detailed annotated version of the 1856 original English Traits text.

Young, Regina Moeller "Endeavours After the Unattainable: The Romantic/Transcendental Quests of Emerson and Hugo (Ralph Waldo Emerson, Victor Hugo, France)" Washington University, 2000, 379 pages—discusses Emerson and Hugo against a backdrop of European Romanticism and American Transcendentalism, using historical, philosophical and cultural aspects.

Books Utilized in this Proposal:

19th Century Books on North Mythology:

Dasent, George Webb B.A. Oxon. "The Prose or Younger Edda Commonly Ascribed to Snorri Sturluson Translated from the Old Norse" Stockholm: Norstedt and Sons, London: William Pickering, 1842.

Laing, Samuel "The Heimskringla; or, Chronicle of The Kings of Norway. Translated from the Icelandic of Snorro Sturleson, With a Preliminary Dissertation" London: Printed for Longman, Brown, Green and Longmans, Paternoster-Row, 1844.

Percy, Bishop, Ed. Blackwell, I.A. "Northern Antiquities; or, An Historical Account of the Manners, Customs, Religion and Laws, maritime Expeditions and Discoveries, Language and Literature of the Ancient Scandinavians, (Danes, Swedes, Norwegians and Icelanders)" Translated from the French of M.Mallet, London: Henry G. Bohn, York Street, Covent Garden, 1847.

Thorpe, Benjamin "Northern Mythology, Comprising the Principal Popular Traditions and Superstitions of Scandinavia, North Germany, and the Netherlands" London: Edward Lumley, Southhampton Street, Bloomsbury Square, 1851-1852.

Examples of Original Sources/Research

May 19, 2005

Ms. Margaret Bancroft
Ralph Waldo Emerson House
28 Cambridge Turnpike
Concord, MA 01742

Dear Ms. Bancroft,

I am writing this letter to request the assistance of you and your acquaintances. My name is Elizabeth Scofield, and I am in the process of writing a Ph.D. with the topic of Ralph Waldo Emerson and his use of Nordic Mythology. This dissertation is being written for Roskilde University in Denmark, however I have spent the past two semesters researching at Harvard University under the guidance of Dr. Lawrence Buell. I have already been in contact with Susan Edwards of the Trustees of Reservations, and with David Wood, Curator for the Concord Museum, both who have agreed to help me in my quest to trace the influence of Nordic Mythology on Ralph Waldo Emerson, specifically to grant me viewing access to manuscripts on the subject housed in their respective institutions.

My request would involve any or all information available linking the Nordic Culture to Mr. Emerson—known influences, books, persons he knew, lessons he was taught. Anything that comes to mind, or directions that I could be pointed in, would be most welcome and helpful.

Thanks so much in advance for your support,

Sincerely,

Elizabeth S. Scofield

Scofield, Elizabeth

From: Scofield, Elizabeth
Sent: Thursday, June 2005 02, 5:21 PM
To: dfwood@concordmuseum.org'
Subject: List of books for viewing for Elizabeth Scofield

Hello David Wood--

I've spoken to you twice on the phone, and am finally sending you the list of books I need to view. There will be more, but these are the most important for now:

1.
Title: Edda of Saemund
Author/Publisher: N.Biggs
Place, Date: Bristol, 1797.

2.
Title: Ancient History (Vol.1-2-3-4-5-6-7-8)
Author/Publisher: Charles Rollins, Munroe & Frances
Place, Date: Boston, 1805

3.
Title: Treatise on Dreams & Visions
Author/Publisher: Thomas Tyron, T. Sowle
Place, Date: London, 1695

4.
Title: Chronology of Ancient Kingdoms
Author/Publisher: Sir Issac Newton
Place, Date: 1728

5.
Title: Elements of History
Author/Publisher: Unknown
Date, Place: Place unknown, 1809

David- there are about 6 more books, But I will start with these.

Fictional Story of Uilsa, daughter of Odin
(written in Emerson's Journal 1820)

98 Uilsa not addressed to me as it seemed but screaming to the woods & the sky "Fall fall scarlet leaves! The trees are my servants to cover me with a royal crimson mantle And am not I a Queen of the woods? I scared the wild eagle at the dawn, for the eye of my mother's daughter was fiercer than his. And who is he," she said, turning suddenly upon me, "who comes to the Cave of the grey Queen Is the spoon or the doublet or the silver or the gold stolen, have their flocks strayed or sickened or is the magistrate come up that they have hunted out Uilsa again?" I was never forcibly impressed and awed with the voice of this woman. When she first turned to me her manner was terrifying but my indignation at being confounded with the ignorant starving rustics who now and then sought her out tended to restore my equilibrium. My instant resolution was to humour her distempered tone of mind and reply to her contemptuous question in similar terms. — "Doth not the Queen of the woods, gather the secrets of futurity when she reads the decaying oak-leaves And can she not tell the young man how to guide his steps in life?" "Have ye come to learn fate then? Your habit is goodly, and the lines of your tenements are fair. But why come to the old and withered hag, the decrepit worm which the people of this land fear and contemn? Though I am thus despised and derided, and have lived in a land which is hateful I did not come from the vulgar dust — Uilsa is highly and proudly descended from an hundred weird women fatal and feared daughters of Odin." She stood up and looked to the north as if expecting a sign in the firmament. I expected one myself. I was awed by this strange character and felt a lively conviction of the truth of her claims to supernatural light. As the Sybil stood up between two blasted oaks glaring on me

(Turn to page 48)

Emerson's thoughts regarding Alfred the Great, who battled against the Danish Vikings. Here, too, he expresses his sentiments towards Sharon Turner (written in Emerson's Journal 1822)

Christmas Dec 23

If, (as with Voltaire) the all that is related of Alfred
the Great be true, I know not the man that ever lived, more
worthy of the gratitude of posterity. I hope the reservation
means nothing. There is not one incredible assertion
made either of his abilities, his character, or his actions,
besides it was not an age, nor were Saxon monks the
men to invent and adorn another Cyropaedia. Though
Turner an ambitious flashing writer, & elsewhere a loose
hath done well by Alfred. His praise rests not upon
monkish eulogy or vague tradition, but upon facts. Some
may quarrel upon the reputed foundation of Oxford it
is not at all necessary to his fame. In the first place
he had the smartest man of his age for his enemy, with
whom he repeatedly constantly & vigorously fought until
he finally drove him utterly from the Kingdom.
Hastings, in despair, retired to France, obtained some
little settlement from the King, where he obscurely
died. The fact, that after his entire loss of every acre of land
& every man of his armies he should be able to reprobate
ab initio his cause & kingdom, equals the Return of Bonaparte. The skilful policy of domesticating the conquered
Danes and thus lulling the opposition of those myriads
which swarmed in Northumbria, and at the same
time creating upon his shores a formidable bulwark to
the future invasions of the sea-kings, by giving their

ALFRED

The Chronicles of Norway say
that in the year 982, Eric the Red, a Nor
wegian youth of noble family sailed from
Iceland with 25 ships, in quest of adventure
& discovery. His fleet took a southwesterly
course & came to a pleasant land full
of lofty timber & offresh & verdant vallies.
Pleased with the beautiful coast, wh. he
called Greenland, Eric resolved to settle there.
After building their houses, they wasted
the short summer in the pursuit ofthe
game wh. was very abundant. But
a summer of unusual mildness was followed
by the stern winter ofthose high latitudes. Their
harbour was frozen & the ill fated colonists
beheld with despair a vast barrier of ice
accumulating on the coast to shut them out
forever, from all communication with
the rest ofthe world. They are supposed to
have perished miserably with cold & famine. The
court of Denmark sent out several ships to
search after the lost Colony. in vain. The sailors
believe the ghosts of the settlers guard the coast & make
all access dangerous

nor the world's law.

a rests here
spent trail
ten palaces
this slave.
on whose foul
wing will stoop, he
was abode. He
clutch, had
ly,
it was.

s Mervinenh
ation
it
see ofthe poor,
Sven stone
destroys
Gibbon
frown,
tion down.

"Vinegar is the Son of Wine."

"Optimus ille animi vindex lædentis pectus,
Vincula qui rupit, dedoluitque semel."

Boston, March 18, 1823.

DEDICATION

When God had made the beasts, & prepared to
set over them an intelligent lord, He considered what
external faculty he should add to his frame, to be the
seal of his superiority. Then He gave him an artic-
ulate Voice. He gave him an organ exquisitely endowed, which was independent of his grosser parts, but
the minister of his mind & the interpreter of its thoughts.
It was designed moreover as a Sceptre of irresistible com-
mand, by whose force, the great & wise should stile the
tumult of the vulgar million, & direct their blind
energies to a right operation. The will of Heaven was
done, & the morning & evening gales wafted to the Highest, the harmonious accents of Man. But the gen-
erations of men lived & died, while yet their expanding

OLD MANSE – PHOTOCOPY INVOICE

ESS
June 11, 2005

Author/ Title: Thomas B. Shaw, William Smith, Henry T. Tuckerman:
A Complete Manual of English Literature (NY: Sheldon & Co 1867)

Page #'s: 5-6, 11-34

pages: 15

ESS
June 11, 2005

Author/ Title: A. Swinton, Travels into Norway, Denmark and Russia in
the Years 1788, 1789, 1790, and 1791 (Dublin: W. Corbet, M.DCC.XCII)

Page #'s: 2, 3, 6, 10, 14, 24 28, 31, 34, 35 36, 37, 38, 39, 40, 41, 42, 43, 46-61, 54-5
60, 61, 63-65, 93, Title, Dedication # pages: 29
x-xiii, bookplate (x3)

ESS
June 17
2005

Author/ Title: David Brewster L.L.D., The American Edition of the New
Edinburgh Encyclopedia (Philadelphia: Edward Parker, 1813) V. IV, Part II

Page #'s: 546, 552

pages: 2

ESS

Author/ Title: Brewster, The American Edition, 1813. V. I, Part I

Page #'s: 395, 396, 397

pages: 3

ESS

Author/ Title: New Edinburgh Encyclopedia -
V. XVII, Part II,

Page #'s: COVER

pages: 1

ESS

Author/ Title: New Edinburgh Encyclopedia (1816) V. VIII, part 2 Emi-Fa

Page #'s: Cover, 415-429

pages: 14

Total # pages: 64

Amount Due (pages x $0.20/page): $12.80

Paid Date: _____

Initials: _____

OLD MANSE – PHOTOCOPY INVOICE

Author/ Title: New Edinburgh Encyclopedia (1814)

Page #'s: Cover

pages: 1

Author/ Title: New Edinburgh Encyclopedia (1815)
V. VII, Pnt 2
Page #'s: Cover, 469, 492, 493, 494, 495, 496, 497

pages: 8

Author/ Title: New Edinburgh Encyclopedia (1832)
V. XVIII, pnt 2
Page #'s: 422, 423

pages: 2

Author/ Title: New Edinburgh Encyclopedia 1823

Page #'s: 520, 521, Cover

pages: 3

Author/ Title: New Edinburgh Encyclopedia 1815
Vol. XIV, Part II   NAV – ORFG
Page #'s: 616,

pages: 1

Author/ Title: New Edinburgh Encyclopedia
V. XI, Pnt 1 HY6 – IRE
Page #'s: Cover, 71, 72, 73

pages: 4

Total # pages: 19

Amount Due (pages x $0.20/page): 3.80

Paid Date: _____

Initials: _____

97

OLD MANSE – PHOTOCOPY INVOICE

Name: Elizabeth Scofield

Author/ Title: New Edinburgh Encyclopedia (1817)
Vox, Part 1   GRA - HER

Page #'s: Cover, 88, 89, 90, 91, 92, 93

pages: 7

ESS

Author/ Title: The Edinburgh Review of Critical Journal, No. XLIX
(N.Y, Eastburn, Kirk, & Co.) June 1815

Page #'s: Cover, 146 - 168

pages: √4

ESS

Author/ Title: Edinburgh Review, No. XLI, Feb. 1813

Page #'s: Cover, 38, 39 40 - 44, 130 - 132, 144, 152, 163

pages: 9

ESS

Author/ Title: Edinburgh Review, NO. XLVIII, Feb. 1815

Page #'s: Cover, 271 276, 282

pages: 4

ESS

Author/ Title: Edinburgh Review, No. LIV, Dec. 1816
Cover, 277 - 279

Page #'s:

pages: 3

ESS

Author/ Title: Edinburgh Review, No. LXXII, Feb. 1822.
Boston; Wells and Lilly

Page #'s: 287 - 312, 321 - 322, Cover.

pages: 17

Total # pages: 54

Amount Due (pages x $0.20/page): 10.80

Paid Date: _____

Initials: _____

Name: _____

85

Author/ Title: David Brewster, LL.D. , New Edinburgh Encyclopedia
Philadelphia ('819)   IRB - LEG
Page #'s: Cover, 458 . 459, 460 , 736, 737, 740
                            # pages: 10

Author/ Title: List of Books in Slug Shed Attic
— Word Document
Page #'s: _____
                            # pages: 5

Author/ Title: Magazin des Cartes et Ouvrages Géographiques:
"Post-Karte von Deutschland" 1843
Page #'s: MAP .
                            # pages: 5

Author/ Title: New Edinburgh Encyclopedia, V. XLI,
Part 1, HYG - IRB
Page #'s: Cover, 84, 85
                            # pages: 3

Author/ Title: New Edinburgh Enc., V. X, Part 7,
GRA — HEN
Page #'s: Cover, 96-97, 104 - 108
                            # pages: 8

Author/ Title: New Edinburgh Enc. V-XIV, Part 2
NAV- ORG , 1823
Page #'s: Cover, 508, 509, 512, 513, 516, 517
                            # pages: 7

Total # pages: 38
Amount Due (pages x $0.20/page): $7.60
Paid Date: _____
Initials: _____

OLD MANSE – PHOTOCOPY INVOICE

Name: _____

Author/ Title: _New Edinburgh Encyclopedia_
V. VII, Part 2, DAI - DJI.

Page #'s: _469, 472 473, 476, 477, 480-81 484-485, 488-89, 492-97,_

pages: _18_

Author/ Title: _Life & Napoleon Bonaparte V. II_
(London C. Roworth Date)

Page #'s: _1 - 4_

pages: _3_

Author/ Title: _J. Britton, The Original Picture of London (London:_
Longman, Rees, Orne, Brown & Green-, ?)

Page #'s: _11 - 27, Cover Pages_

pages: _6_

Author/ Title: _Dr. Goldsmith, History of England, 1838-_

Page #'s: _Cover Plate, 11 - 23_

pages: _9_

Author/ Title: _D.R. Preston, The Wonders of Creation, 1907_

Page #'s: _Cover, 2 inside leaves, 5-6, 177-179_

pages: _7_

Author/ Title: _W. M. Cunning, Introduction To Ethics_

Page #'s: _Cover, 113 -144_

pages: _7_

Total # pages: _60_

Amount Due (pages x $0.20/page): _$12.50_

Paid Date: _____

Initials: _____

1

OLD MANSE – PHOTOCOPY INVOICE

Name: _____

Author/ Title: Alexander Ross A View of All
& Religions in the World

Page #'s: Cover Plate, 106 - 109

pages: 4

Author/ Title: D'Anville, Compendium of Ancient Geography.

Page #'s: Covel, xiv - xxvii, 98-99, 120-125

pages: 12

Author/ Title: Harvard Register 1827 - 28

Page #'s: Cover, 12-13, 16, 17, 22, 94-106, 123-124, 177-182, 224, 333-336, 380-382

pages: 25

Author/ Title: An Abridgment of The History of England, Dr. Goldsmith

Page #'s: Cover, 8-9, 12-27

pages: 10

Author/ Title: A View of Religions in 2 Parts by Hannah Adams

Page #'s: Covel, 302-325, 332-335

pages: 5

Author/ Title: David Hume Esq, The History of England

Page #'s: Title, 14-15, 30, 50, 56-75, 98, 109-118, 521-522, back plate

pages: 23

Edinborough Review Covers, Travels in Sicily ~ 30 pages = 6.00

Total # pages: 79

Amount Due (pages x $0.20/page): $15.80

Paid Date: 7/20/05

Initials: J.I.D

TOTAL $12.80 + $3.80 + $10.80 + $7.60 + $12.00 + $15.80 = 62.80
+ 6 —
68.80

101

TRAVELS

INTO

NORWAY, DENMARK,

AND

RUSSIA.

IN THE

YEARS 1788, 1789, 1790, AND 1791.

BY

A. SWINTON, Esq.

DUBLIN:

PRINTED BY W. CORBET,

FOR W. JONES, DAME-STREET, AND J. RICE, COLLEGE-GREEN.

M,DCC,XCII.

William Emerson.

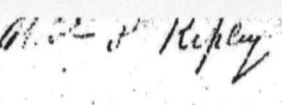

THE

EDINBURGH REVIEW,

OR

CRITICAL JOURNAL:

(N° LXXII.)

FEBRUARY, 1822.

TO BE CONTINUED QUARTERLY.

JUDEX DAMNATUR CUM NOCENS ABSOLVITUR.
PUBLIUS SYRUS.

BOSTON:

PUBLISHED BY WELLS AND LILLY.
....
1822.

☞ The (LONDON) QUARTERLY, or EDINBURGH REVIEW,
will be sent to any part of the UNITED STATES, by mail, upon
the Publishers receiving a remittance of one year's subscrip-
tion. ($5)

A

VIEW OF RELIGIONS,

IN TWO PARTS.

PART I. CONTAINING AN ALPHABETICAL COMPENDIUM
OF THE VARIOUS

RELIGIOUS DENOMINATIONS,

WHICH HAVE APPEARED IN THE WORLD, FROM THE
BEGINNING OF THE CHRISTIAN ERA TO
THE PRESENT DAY.

PART II. CONTAINING A BRIEF ACCOUNT OF
THE DIFFERENT SCHEMES OF RELIGION
NOW EMBRACED AMONG MANKIND.

THE WHOLE COLLECTED
From the best AUTHORS, Ancient and Modern.

BY HANNAH ADAMS.

The SECOND EDITION, *with large* ADDITIONS.

Prove all things, hold fast that which is good. Apostle PAUL.

BOSTON:
PRINTED BY JOHN WEST FOLSOM.

DD HUME
Esq.

Campbell's Edition of Hume's History of England

THE
HISTORY
OF
ENGLAND,

FROM THE

INVASION OF JULIUS CÆSAR

TO

THE REVOLUTION IN MDCLXXXVIII.

IN SIX VOLUMES, ILLUSTRATED WITH PLATES.

BY DAVID HUME, Esq.

A NEW EDITION, WITH THE AUTHOR'S LAST COR-
RECTIONS AND IMPROVEMENTS.

TO WHICH IS PREFIXED

A SHORT ACCOUNT OF HIS LIFE, WRITTEN BY HIMSELF.

VOL. I.

PHILADELPHIA:

PRINTED FOR ROBERT CAMPBELL:
BY SAMUEL H. SMITH.
M,DCC,XCV.

"Orig. inhab - ||cesar.
55 Rom. Conquest ||61 Lond. Burnt
448 ' ' leave \\ Picts + Scots
450 Saxons Hengist + Horsa
Votegern + Vortimer
150 yrs contest
827 Egbert
871:901 Alfred
1017 Canute
Harold
Hardicanute
1042
Ed. Confessor 1041-66
Roman 400
Saxon (Heptarchy 400)
600
(Urig 200) (This word is illegible)

50"

orig. inhab — *Cæsar.*

55 *Rom. conquest*　61 Lond. burnt

448 　"　　Leave

450 Saxons Hengist + 20 Sea

　　　・ Watigen + Vortimer

　　　　150 years combat

827 Egbert　　871: 901 Ælfred

1017 Canute

　　Harold

　　Har. & Canute

1043

Ed. Confessor 1041 – 66

Norman it —
Saxon (Hist. books 400) 600
　　(Hist. vers.)

　　50

"To showcase an additional example, a leaf found on the page of Saxony and Scandinavia in an Encyclopaedia Britannica had been there for so long that an imprint of the leaf was now permanently stained on the page."

ters, which have been found principally in the lofty-range of the Erzegebirge. The basis of this range is granite, upon which rest gneiss, mica and clay slate. Basalt in regular columns occur in various parts. There are a few silver mines here. Iron is found in the primitive mountains, and copper and lead in the secondary ones. Arsenic, cobalt, tin, cinnabar, mercury, bismuth, antimony, &c. are also found. Among the valuable stones, are topazes, amethysts, chrysolites, garnets, tourmalines, and all the varieties of the quartz family, such as agates, cornelians, &c. The porcelain earth found in the neighbourhood of Meissen gave rise to the celebrated porcelain manufactory of Meissen, which we have already described in our article PORCELAIN.

Saxony has long possessed extensive manufactories of woollen goods; and the weaving of linen is carried on to a great extent. At Chemnitz, Plauen, &c. cotton spinning is extensively carried on. Leipsic contains some silk manufactures. In our articles CHEMNITZ, DRESDEN, and LEIPSIC, will be found an account of various other Saxon manufactures.

Freiberg is a town highly interesting for its institutions and manufactures connected with the rivers of the district. There is here a mining academy, of which M. Mohs is now professor, having succeeded to Werner. Connected with that institution, there is a cabinet of minerals and of natural history. There is here a manufacture of false lace, carried on by M. Thiele, and occupying 1000 persons. The 103 mines wrought in the canton of Freiberg yielded in 1749, 49,714 marcs of coined silver, and in 1800, 45,949.

The net produce of all the Saxon Erzegebirge from 1761 to 1801, amounted to 22,447,738 rix-dollars. The house of Amalgamation is about a league from Freiberg. About 60,000 quintals of ore yield here from 28,000, to 30,000 marcs of silver, and there are laid up annually for the use of that establishment 10,000 voies of wood. See *La Description de tous les Travaux tant d'amalgamation que de fonderie qui sont en usage dans les atteliers de Halsbruck pres de Freiberg, par M. Fragoso de Sigueiro.* Dresden 1800.

The want of inland communication is unfavourable to the trade of the kingdom, the ordinary method of transport being by waggon, and the roads being in general not good. The principal articles of export are wool, linen, and woollen goods, yarn, tar, and minerals. The chief articles imported are silk, flax, cotton, coffee, sugar, wine, and corn in plentiful seasons.

Although the royal family of Saxony are Catholics, having abjured the doctrines of the Reformation in 1697, in order to obtain the crown of Poland, yet there is a great majority of Lutherans in the population. The Catholics indeed amount only to 40,000. Leipsic is now the only university seat in Saxony. The establishments for education are numerous, and under good regulations, and the lower classes are in general taught reading and writing. There are endowed classical schools at Meissen, Wurzen, Grimma, &c.

In Saxony the sovereign shares the legislative power with the states. The states consist of two houses, the one being formed of the bishops and nobility, and the other of landholders and deputies from towns. There is here a cabinet council, a board of finance, a military court of appeal, and an upper ecclesiastical court.

The revenue of Saxony has been estimated at one million and a quarter sterling. The public debt is £3,700,000 sterling, and the military force on the peace establishment, 10,000.

The following are the principal towns in Saxony, with their present population.

Town	Population	Town	Population
Dresden,	50,000	Schneeberg,	4,500
Leipsic,	33,000	Annaberg,	4,300
Chemnitz,	11,000	Hennersdorf,	4,300
Bautzen,	11,000	Eylau,	4,300
Freiberg,	10,500	Zwickau,	4,000
Zittau,	7,200	Dobeln,	4,000
Plauen,	6,000	Tschopa,	3,800
Meissen,	6,000	Perna,	3,800
Ebersbach,	5,000	Grimma,	3,000
Mittweyda,	5,000		

The history of Saxony has been so much interwoven with that of the other nations of Europe, that we must refer our readers for a farther account of it to our articles ANGLO-SAXONS, AUSTRIA, BRITAIN, ECCLESIASTICAL *History*, FRANCE, &c.

SAYPAN. See LADRONES.

SCALES. See ARITHMETIC.

SCALES. See DRAWING INSTRUMENTS, and NAVIGATION.

SCALIGER, JULIUS CÆSAR, a celebrated scholar, and the author of various learned works distinguished more by their erudition than by any marks of genius. He was born at Verona in 1484, and he died in 1558, in the 75th year of his age. His treatise *De Arte Poetica*, which appeared in 1561, and his philosophical work *De Causis Linguæ Latinæ*, which was published in 1540, are the ablest of his productions.

SCALIGER, JOSEPH JUSTUS, the son of the subject of the preceding article, was born at Agen in 1540, and died at Leyden in 1609, at the age of 69. He was a man of great learning, and was acquainted with thirteen languages. His principal work *De Emendatione Temporum*, which first appeared at Paris in 1587, contains a complete system of chronology, founded on fixed principles. His *Thesaurus Temporum* is a sort of supplement to that work. It appeared in 1658, in 2 vols. folio. Scaliger invented the Julian period.

SCALPA, a small island of the Hebrides, between the Isle of Skye and the mainland. It i[s] single mountain, the base of which is abou[t] long, and from two to three broa[d]

SCAMMONY. See CHEMISTRY, [ME-]DICA.

SCANDINAVIA. See [SWEDEN.]

SCAPOLITE. See [MINERALOGY.]

SCARABEUS. See ENTOMOLO[GY, ARTICLE]

SCARBA, an island of the Hebrides, lying between Jura and Lunga. It is of a circular shape, and above three and a half miles in diameter, resembling a single mountain, which rises to the height of 1500 feet. A narrow strait divides it from Lunga, and it is separated from Jura by the famous whirlpool of Corrybhreaccan, which we have already fully described in our account of JURA. Scarba contains about fifty inhabitants.

SCARBOROUGH, a sea port and market town of England, in the North Riding of Yorkshire. The

(Author's Note: British spellings and a few extra spaces exist here; the end notes are also not formalized. This is the student submitted paper with all of that intended to be formalized at a later time.)

How the Scandinavian Stories
Influenced the Thought
Development of
Ralph Waldo Emerson
2005

How the Scandinavian Stories Influenced the thought development of Ralph Waldo Emerson

Proof that R.W.Emerson knew about the Scandinavian Self-Reliant Trait long before he wrote the essay entitled Self-Reliance.

Section One: Introduction

Section Two: Literary Review
Works on the sources for Emerson's Self-Reliance Theory, documenting the absent inclusion of Scandinavia, specifically Viking age (and previous era) and inherent traits
Works on Emerson and Race, as close to the Scandinavian issue as possible
Works on Emerson and England
Refute: Works that suggest Emerson was unaffected by Scandinavian influences
Works that suggest Thomas Carlyle was the first to introduce Emerson to the Viking Period

Section Three: Methodology
Include:
Personal Letter from Dr.Buell, acceptance for appointment at Harvard
Hand-written letter from Philip Nicoloff
Personal Letter from Dr. Christoph Irmscher
Personal Letter from Bay Bancroft, descendant of Ralph Waldo Emerson
Document lack of response from Dr. Burkholder

Section Four: Sources from the Old Manse

> March 6, 1823
> My brother Edward asked me whether I have a right to make use of animals? I answered "yes" and shall attempt to give my reasons. A poor native of <Greenland> Lapland found himself in mid winter destitute of food, clothing, and light, and without even a bow to <procure> defend himself from the beasts. In this perplexity he met with a reindeer which he killed & conveyed to his hut. He now found himself supplied with oil to light his lamp, with a warm covering for his

> body & with wholesome & strengthening food, and with bowstrings withal, whereby he could again procure a similar supply."[i]

This quote is taken from Emerson's journals, when he was 19 years old. In it, he uses a Scandinavian to demonstrate a simplified use of self-reliance. The proper name Greenland is crossed out in the journals, and Lapland is the replacement for it. The man in the example identifies his requirements of food clothing, light, and weapon, in order to defend himself as well as to, most importantly, maintain the course of action—finding a reindeer and slaying it—to continue to furnish his needs in order to survive in the north. This becomes significant because in one of the encyclopedias that Emerson was exposed to as a child, this near exact scene has been described.[ii] Here is an example of a practical definition of self-reliance: depending on one oneself for provisions of one's necessities.

The above journal entry certainly demonstrates the self-reliance of the Laplander, and Emerson's idea that they are an innocuous race. {The line, "Does any mind question the innocence of this starving wretch in thus giving life and comfort to a desolate family in that polar corner of the world?" follows the quote above).[iii] However, this view of innocence of the entire population of Scandinavians does not stay consistent throughout the entries in his journals. What does stay consistent is his draw for those of this region, the time period of the Viking age and before (and the mythology that they worshipped) and of the traits that was carried along with them.

The question I want to answer primarily is from whence this fascination, influence and admiration for the Viking-age Scandinavians came? Fortunately, the evidence makes the answer rather clear, after viewing the library owned by his family. Numerous sources provide the background that comprehensibly links his childhood exposure to the Scandinavian activities, beliefs and values, and what is written by Emerson in his journals beginning at age 17, when the journals that survive begin. Furthermore, there is physical evidence that these pages describing the Scandinavians and their traits have actually been sought out and read.

The family library provided an excellent source of explicit detailing of the Scandinavians and their traits, in this collection of books, literary reviews, and encyclopedias with dates corresponding to Emerson's childhood. These books are found in the Old Manse, the house built in Concord by Emerson grandfather, William, and afterwards owned by Emerson's step-grandfather, Ezra Ripley, who had married Emerson's widowed grandmother, Phebe. Emerson's father, also named William, was the second child of the original five of Phebe's brood (she produced three more children during her marriage to Ezra) and was brother to Mary Moody, who helped raise Ralph Waldo Emerson after the death of his father. William Emerson, a minister, died on his way home from war when Ralph Waldo was just eight years old, thereby leaving, one can assume, an empty hole and a lasting impression upon the young boy.

Before going further, one must have a clear view of Ralph Waldo's atmosphere and upbringing in order to understand why the Scandinavian independent and self-reliant philosophy and values might be so acutely interesting to him, and his family. At Ralph Waldo's birth in 1803, the United States of America was officially 27 years old. The entire premise of the United States breaking away from Great Britain and becoming a country in itself was based on the idea that the people living in America wanted to provide for themselves, take care of themselves, govern themselves in their own ways and make their own decisions—in essence, become a self-reliant country. The residents wanted to manager their own affairs, and flourish within their own laws, ideas and production. Emerging as a young country, America was trying to make a go of it, proud and determined to succeed on its own, naming the annual celebration of this event "Independence Day".

However, this does not do the explanation justice of why the Emerson and Ripley family in particular was zealously dedicated to this concept. What is not widely advertised (and in my opinion, unquestionably should be) is that the revolution of the American Colonies began on Ralph Waldo's grandfather's land. The 'shot heard round the world', as Ralph Waldo himself wrote in his tribute to the dispute years later for a dedication of the event, occurred merely steps away from the Old Manse; the skirmish was in full view from the house. One can clearly see the spot of the first resistance from the study in the second floor window, and can imagine the family, Ralph Waldo's father included, gathered there in anxious apprehension watching the small yet significant battle taking place down on the bridge below. Ezra Ripley had assisted in the organization of the resistance against the British forces, and without delving into a lengthy historical account of his activities here (further reading is provided in the end bibliography), he undoubtedly carried with him a strong sense of independent spirit and self-reliance all his own, which was logically absorbed by his family. It is little wonder, then, that there are several unmistakable particulars proving that interest in the Nordic Culture was among the Emerson clan. An oakleaf was placed as a marker pointing to the word "Scandinavia" in the New Edinburgh Encyclopedia of 1829, and had been there long enough to leave a deep stained outline of the leaf (both leaf and stain were present when I opened the book to the page). In the 1815 Edition of the Edinburgh Review, at the beginning section of the explanation of the Nordic mythology used in a featured poem, the page corner is turned down. Were this a common occurrence in the Edinburgh Reviews that are in the family collection at the Old Manse, this finding would not carries the weight that it does; However this was one of the only pages I discovered with the corner turned down in the entire set. In the various encyclopedias from 1812 to 1823 portraying the numerous aspects of the Scandinavians, such as lifestyle, landscapes, values, mythology and mannerisms, several pages had been cleanly cut from the top, (whereas the majority of the pages were still connected to one another) indicating that the person reading them felt their contents important enough to have easier visual access to the information these pages contained.

It is difficult to discern from some of the collection which book was owned by whom in the Emerson family, regardless of the date of publication that puts the manuscript into the timeframe of Ralph Waldo's youth. Nevertheless, certain evidences can narrow down the original owner of the book or manuscript. Several of the books have names written in them, or dedications made from one person to another. Many of the Edinburgh Reviews have Ezra Ripley's name handwritten across the top of the front cover in black ink. However, in this collection, one such book stood out as representing a key aspect to solving the puzzle. This book is entitled, *Travels into Norway, Denmark, and Russia, in the Years 1788, 1789, 1790, and 1791,* by Andrew Swinton. We know it belonged specifically to William Emerson, Ralph Waldo's father, from two sources; firstly, his book plate is on the inside cover of the book (see Appendix) and, with no additional handwriting anywhere on the plate indicating that Mary Moody Emerson was using the bookplate for her own purposes as conveyed in *Mary Moody Emerson and the Origins of Transcendentalism,* by Phillis Cole. The second source is an official 1822 notice of the collection of William Emerson's books to be sold at Auction that contains this very same book on the list, thereby verifying that the book is indeed the property of William Emerson the second.[iv]

This particular book proves to be invaluable as to discovering the source of exposure regarding the Scandinavians during Ralph Waldo's youth because of its 1792 publishing date-- it places the book at the starting point, in terms of both time period and content. This book tells quite a lot about what the Scandinavians were experts in, and what they accomplished, how the countries were connected and their exploits. For example, the paragraph on page six states,

> The Norwegians very early
> distinguished themselves in naval

> expeditions; but unfortunately they have only retained their conquests in the north. They planted colonies in Iceland and Greenland, and from a part of these colonists are descended the Esquimaux who dwell upon the dreary coasts of Labradore. Sometimes under the Kings of their own, sometimes under the Danish Monarchs, they frequently invaded England, Scotland, and Ireland. Denmark, during her former greatness, ruling over Sweden, and all the kingdoms around the Baltic; the name and actions of the Norwegians were lost in that of the Danes. At this day, Norway is the only remain of all the Danish conquests...[v]

Other paragraphs go more explicitly into the actual lifestyle, attitudes, old religion and accomplishments of the Scandinavians, as will be related to later on, however this particular paragraph not only exposes that it was Denmark that was the famed country of exploits no matter which actual Nordic region the adventurers hailed from, but, most importantly for this study, it introduces the invasions of the British Isles that were made by the Scandinavians, and these invasions turn up several times in the journals, as well as in published writings; The manuscript *English Traits* being one of them. Since this is a study of influences of the Scandinavians upon Emerson in specific reference to the self-reliance theory and characteristics that go along with that theory, I will leave out the later writings, and focus only on what was written and produced before 1841, the publication date of the essay *Self-Reliance*.

However, this section concerning the evidence found at the Old Manse will cover only those manuscripts available to him as a child and young adult, to lay a foundation of viable interest for him, since this would be chronologically Emerson's first contact with who and what the Scandinavians were. The section following this one, Section 5, will cover all other sources up until the year 1835, since this is the date of the lecture series of Emerson 's on English Literature, which includes the lecture *Permanent Traits of the English National Genius* In which much of the content is based on The Scandinavian stories and traits, referring to Sharon Turner's *History of the Anglo-Saxons*—this has been previously documented with the publication of the lecture series.[vi] Therefore it is my aim to document what Emerson's exposure up until that lecture was as well, and why it made such an impact on him. Clearly, if his family was interested in the Scandinavians and their characteristics and mannerisms, as well as their connection to England, this would have made a huge impact on him—and would have been reiterated once again when using material that covered the same topic in a public lecture.

Every author in the collection touching upon the Scandinavians in some way that I came across used words that undeniably exposed the descriptor's high regard for these people, regardless if their activities were farming, exploring, or negotiating. Uncannily, even when there is a negative aspect to point out, the authors still describe the people of Scandinavia, regardless of section, as "ingenious" – often multiple times in one article. Thus, the admiration for them must have been catching to the reader as well—and Emerson was no exception. Although his style of writing was more observant than opinionated for the most part, evidence of his fascination of the Scandinavians is clear, weaving them into original poetry, fictional writings, judgmental commentaries on the writings of Sharon Turner regarding King Alfred (long before his 1835 lecture) and general snippets that seems simply stuck in there—such as the account of Eric the Red discovering Greenland, founding a settlement there then perishing with the rest of the colonists because their harbour had been iced in—written on the back of a scrap of paper and wax-glued into the journal. Even Madame de Stael, a French writer that is known to have been read by Emerson because of the multitudes of references to her in his journals, is chronicled in the 1813 edition of the Edinburgh Review to have agreed that the Scandinavians have genius, however simply have want of taste and don't know how to use it. The reviewer of her article defends even this slight bit of negativity towards the Scandinavians, adding in regards to Ms. De Stael's comments "that what is called want of taste, is merely excess of genius and independence of pedantic rules and authorities."[vii]

Evidence

Moving forward to relate this topic directly to Ralph Waldo Emerson, I would like to draw attention first and foremost to a paragraph from *Swinton's Travels,* and is a passage which describes, in words, the Self-Reliance of the Scandinavian people:

> The Norwegians are a fine race of men, of a free and generous spirit, and watch over their liberties with unremitted vigilance. Many ages have elapsed since they have settled quietly at home, and ceased to disturb the liberty of others. The Norwegians are all husbandmen, fishermen, or mariners. There are few other distinct professions among them: *every one, as is commonly the case in northern countries in general, is his own tailor, carpenter, shoemaker, smith, &c.* They show much ingenuity in every thing they undertake; and some of the greatest curiosities in the Royal Museum at Copenhagen are the handy-works of Norwegian peasants.[viii](my italics)

For the Scandinavians, there was no need to depend on a specialist, such as a cobbler, to be certain that their feet were shod; they each learned to perform this duty for themselves. The Northerners learned the skills to survive, and have their needs met, for each person on an individual basis. When a solution to a situation was not already in place, they used their inventiveness and creativity to construct one, and every situation was an

opportunity to create another solution, and continue on with living—

another aspect attributed to the Scandinavians by several writers.

What makes this particular paragraph even more notable is that

there is a section in the essay of *Self-Reliance* that has a similar

tone to it:

> A sturdy lad from New Hampshire
> or Vermont, who in turn tries all the
> professions, who *teams it*, *farms it*,
> *peddles*, keeps a school, preaches,
> edits a newspaper, goes to
> Congress, buys a township, and so
> forth, in successive years, and
> always, like a cat, falls on his feet,
> is worth a hundred of these city
> dolls. He walks abreast with his
> days, and feels no shame in not
> 'studying a profession,' for he does
> not postpone his life, but lives
> already. He has not one chance,
> but a hundred chances. [ix]

There could be several reasons why Emerson puts a statement like

that in an essay possessing the concept he refers to as one he

spent most of his life attempting to relay to others, but the fact that

he was shown explicitly how the self-reliance philosophy could work

in real life by a cluster of countries that have survived and thrived

practicing just that, unquestionably influenced his thought process

and personal philosophy. Just by this comparison alone, it is

evident that there was some influence. However, one must look at

the specific sources in detail that the Old Manse yielded.

The characteristic of the Northerners have across the board been noted as self-reliant. To take the case of the Laplanders up once again, there is a passage in the 1819 New Edinburgh Encyclopedia, in the collection of his grandfather Ripley, which would have been accessible to Ralph Waldo when he was sixteen years old:

> From the horns of the rein-deer (sic) they manufacture spoons in a very neat manner, which they stain with figures tolerably well designed. With no other instrument than a knife, they also carve their bowls and spoons with wonderful expertness. The steel of these knives they manufacture for themselves, and ornament in a style of some elegance.[x]

The preface to *The Compendium of Ancient Geography* includes a paragraph that pinpoints associative characteristics of the Scandinavians that were traits Emerson held in high esteem, and points to the Scandinavians as one of the first examples to him that would not only carry these traits, but implement them as well, relying on only themselves to do so:

> In the year 874, a colony under the conduct of a hero named Ingulph, braving the utmost rigour of the elements, settled in the uninhabited and volcanic island of Iceland; and thereby exhibited an example the most admirable upon record, of

what human genius, courage, and perseverance can achieve. For in a land scarcely habitable through the eternal conflict between Fire and Ice, they digested a wise and equal government, and became not more distinguished for an implacable enmity to tyrants, than for the successful cultivation of every species of polite literature.[xi]

The Norwegians are highlighted once again in the Edinburgh

Encyclopedia, Section Norway:

The character of the Norwegians as a people is more interesting, and estimable than that of most other nations. Their expressions are clear and energetic, their answers distinct and correct, their questions pertinent and judicious, their reflections often profound and intelligent, beyond what could be imagined in their limited opportunities of education. There is a generosity of heart and elevation of mind about them, which gives their manners a very frank and decided stamp. They speak and act in the spirit of free men, open and undaunted, yet never insolent in the presence of their superiors...In some of the cities, there is a cultivated style of conversation, and polish of manners, mixed with the high and independent spirit of the nation, which form altogether an accomplished character, not to be expected in the remote latitudes and limited advantages of Scandinavia.[xii]

Sir George Mackenzie, a famed traveller of the late 18th century

and early 19th century, after declaring that "every Icelander, of whatever rank, can shoe a horse"[xiii] was also impressed at how many of the basic needs were taken care of by each Icelander for themselves at home. He had this to say about the Icelanders in his book *Travels in Iceland, during the Summer of the year 1810,* as related in the Edinburgh Review of 1812:

> Everything, such as weaving, spinning, knitting, forging horse-shoes, &c. is done at home, and forms the household work in the long dismal winter of this climate. The extent of the home manufacturing is doubtless why clothing is a part of the wages of labour: such articles, in many of the situations in Iceland, cannot be had easily for purchase.[xiv]

The review of Madame De Stael's works in the 1813 Edinburgh Review as mentioned previously clearly declares,

> Another characteristic is the hereditary independence of the Northern tribes—arising partly from their scattered population and inaccessible retreats and partly from the physical force and hardihood which their way of life, and the exertions requisite to procure subsistence, necessarily produced. Their religious creed, too, even before their conversion to Christianity, was less fantastic, and more capable of leading to heroic emotions than that of the southern nations. The respect and

> tenderness with which they always regarded their women, is another cause (or effect) of the peculiarity of their national character.....there are certain savage virtues that can scarcely exist in perfection in a state of complete civilization, and as specimens at least, we may wish to preserve and be allowed to admire them, with all of their acceptable accomplishments. [xv]

The author of the review attempts to put forth that it is the Protestant religion that would be the main cause for many aspects of the characteristics of the Northern people, however this is not supported in any of the other documents I have read regarding the matter,[xvi] nor is it the view of Madame De Stael herself, as she plainly writes her admiration for a people with "hereditary independence" which, scientifically, hasn't anything to do with a newly-converted to religion, not to mention her declaration of the "savage virtues" that should be preserved, indicating that independence be one of them. One can safely assume that Emerson agreed with her views on this matter.

An additional reviewer in the June 1815 edition of the Edinburgh Review, No. XLIX, agrees with the sentiments of Madam De Stael, concerning the review of William Herbert's poem *Helga*. Although the reviewer has some thoughts of his own regarding the author ("Mr. Herbert has taken some pains to show that he is a freethinker, and an unbeliever in the Edda"[xvii]) he does go one step further than

Ms. De Stael in declaring the connection of the Scandinavians with

the then modern population, declaring,

> Less daring than the flights of
> Southey or Lord Byron is the
> attempt of Mr. Herbert to avail
> himself of the mythology of the
> North…besides which, it is
> familiarized, at least in our opinion,
> by its nationality. We cannot forget
> that we are grafts of the old stock.
> The accents and tones of the Norse
> tongue, vibrate upon our ears
> whenever we pass through he
> threshold of the door. Every week
> of our lives we are visited by Thor,
> Woden, and Freya. And although
> the Dane-gelt may have left no
> grateful recollections amongst our
> Southern fellow subjects, yet they
> may become somewhat reconciled
> to the fictions of the Volsunga
> Saga, when they are reminded, that
> our liberties were at length secured
> by calling in the posterity of
> Brynhilda. [xviii]

The Dane-gelt was the money demanded by the Danish society

living in England just before and at the time of King Alfred, in order

to ensure that they would not violently harass the native British

citizens, and ensuing against further attacks from other Viking

parties. The reviewer also manifests by quoting the preface to

William Herbert's *Helga* that "'by undertaking an original poem, of

which the scene is should be laid amongst the Scandinavians, he

should be able to illustrate their manners, religion and superstitions,

in a form that would be more pleasing to the reader.'"[xix]

Whether or not the manners, religion and superstitions of the Scandinavians were indeed illustrated in a pleasing form in this poem is not a subject upon which I will spend time discussing, however it is significant to note that on the page that these two passages are taken from, -- the page corner is turned down. It is the only page corner turned down in this entire volume of the Edinburgh Review. One of the Emerson or Ripley family thought it important enough to mark for later, perhaps to show to another family member, a friend, an acquaintance, or to come back to review for his or herself. Regardless, it is a physical piece of evidence that the people of the Nordic countries and their ways was unquestionably a significant topic within the Emerson/Ripley family unit.

Chronology

The most sensible approach to revealing what the Old Manse has in its collection regarding this topic and how it relates to the influence on Emerson's self-reliant theory is to do so chronologically through historical time, and thematically as well. The grounds for this lay in a hand-written list found at the back of the book of David Hume's *History of England*, which was published in 1795. There is no personalized inscription for the book nor bookplate to directly identify the owner within the family; However, because of its publication date, we can safely assume the close

proximity of the book to Ralph Waldo during his childhood. What

makes this hand-written list so special is that it chronicles the

history of England *with specifically those individuals and events that*

involved contact with the Scandinavians. The list transpires exactly

as follows:

```
Orig.  inhab  -           ||cesar.
55     Rom. Conquest              ||61 Lond. Burnt
448           ' '           leave   \\ Picts + Scots
450    Saxons              Hengist + Horsa
Votegern + Vortimer
150 yrs contest
827   Egbert
871:901 Alfred
1017 Canute
Harold
Hardicanute
1042
Ed. Confessor 1041-66
Roman 400
Saxon (Heptarchy 400)
600
(Urig                     200)   (This word is illegible)
50
```

I will provide an unofficial explanation to this list: original inhabitants

of the island of Britain were here when Ceasar arrived, as he

reported them; Roman conquest of England occurred in 55 AD, and

in 61 AD the newly-built city of London was burnt down by the

Celtic tribe of Iceni, led by their Queen Boudicca . The Picts and the

Scots were battling in the Northern part of England, and in 448 AD

the Romans left Britain. In 449, to aid the Southern Britons against the attacks of the Northern Picts, the Saxons came over the channel, led by Hengist and Horsa, two princes who were brothers and reputed to be descendents of Odin, the Head deity of Nordic Mythology. Vortigern was King of the Britons who invited the Saxons over to help them defend themselves against the Picts and the Scots, and Vortimer was his son. Then there was a 150 year struggle within England and the result was the Heptarchy: seven Saxon kingdoms of Kent, Sussex, Wessex, East Anglia, Mercia, Essex, and Northumberland that were established in Britain.[xx]. In 827 King Egbert came onto the united kingdoms' throne, and five years later the Danish Vikings begin attacks on the western shores, rendering England, years later, in ruins. King Alfred ruled England in 871 until 901, bringing peace to both the inhabiting Danish Community and the English community under one rule. In 1017 Canute, the Danish King, ruled England under Danish sovereignty. At his death in 1035, Harold his son was given England to rule, and his other son Hardicanute was given Denmark. Edward the Confessor, the Nephew of Canute, ruled from 1041 until 1066, when William of Hastings (France) crossed the channel and took over England. The Romans attempted to rule in 400, the Saxons (Heptarchy in 400, and an illegible name in 200), and both adding up to 600 – assuming these numbers represent years in history. The 50 on the bottom of the page is a bit of a mystery; however, the rest of the list is clear enough, and give a very good base to prove where the fascination for the Self-Reliance of the Scandinavians

stems from.

To prove a point, I will start out with a quote from Emerson's

journals, then backtrack a bit in historical sequence before pushing

forward. From Emerson's journals:

> The fierce savages of Asia broke in.
> They too had a mythology. They
> had a war-like heaven, a paradise
> of the strong, a glorified
> gymnasium, fresh air, fine horses,
> robust health and good game—
> filled up to their brim all their
> conception of well-being. Blood and
> thunder in the background of
> Vallhalla. [xxi]

Aside from the word of Vallhalla referring to the resident hall of

Odin, the Scandinavian All father in Nordic Mythology, The

Edinburgh Encyclopedia's section of Norway distinctly states that

the Norwegian horses are "small, well-proportioned, lively, hardy,

and often extremely beautiful" as well as describing the Norwegian

children as "robust and healthy" .[xxii] Andrew Swinton in his *Travels*

defines the Norwegians as "celebrated for their longitvity, and a

hardy strong constitution, both of body and mind."[xxiii] And finally,

Emerson himself in his journals repeats this sentiment:

> If we were to continue the
> personification, we might

> say she (nature) acted like
> a wise parent in mingling
> the Northern nations with
> the South that the
> hardihood of those might
> be softened <with> by the
> refinements of these. [xxiv]

This being established, the detail to note in the first quote is the

introductory sentence, "The fierce savages of Asia broke in." Snorri

Sturluson, the writer of the *Heimskringla, History of the Kings of*

Norway, was not the only person to pen down the idea that the

original Scandinavians came from Asia, although he may have

been one of the more well-known to do so. Currently disputed and

even ridiculed among modern scholars, apparently in Emerson's

time this idea was not only accepted, but standard fare, since within

the collection at the Old Manse there are several authors with this

view. It is stated blatantly in the book *The Wonders of Creation,* by

D.R. Preston published in 1807, "Laws, arts, sciences, and religion,

almost all had their origin in Asia"[xxv].The authors seem to have

various ideas about how the tribes actually arrived in Scandinavia,

either directly or indirectly through Germany, and indeed, the

details conflict of how the Asian tribes became involved in the

British Isles.[xxvi] All agree, however, that these tribes were known as

the Scythians, or Goths, who later became the Saxons-- who in turn

had driven out the Celts from these lands. In the Edinburgh

Encyclopedia section of Norway, it states that "the ancient

inhabitants of Norway are supposed to have been a colony of the

Basterna, a numerous and powerful Gothic tribe, but according to Pliny, Strabo, and Tacitus, they were rather of German extraction."[xxvii] With the references to the Roman figure, this ties in nicely with the handwritten list at the back of David Hume's book (there are also references to the Romans knowing about the Scandinavians in Hume's book as well). However, logically, since the Scythians, or Goths, physically ousted the Celts from these lands, this would mean that the Asian tribes were not, actually, the first bloodline of the Scandinavian lands-- the Celts were. Even Andrew Swinton agrees with this: "Skaw is a low land forming the north point of Jutland, the ancient Cimbrica Chersonesus, from whence issued that hive of people called Angles, who conquered England, and gave their name to our country."[xxviii]

The *Compendium of Ancient Geography*, by Monsieur D'Anville published in 1814—which would have made Ralph Waldo eleven years old— is begun with a preface by the translator. He explains that the primary people, the Celts, were further subdivided into the Gaels, or Celts proper, and the Cimbri (also spelled Cymbri or Cimmmerii) , a name which Emerson mentions in his journals. The explanation continues on to describe the Cimbri as the "inhabitants of Jutland and Denmark" that may or may not have been Germanic. This becomes important later on. The following paragraph, however, must have made quite an impression on a young boy with developing ideas about ethnic, cultural and national heritage:

It is premised then that all of Europe, from the Baltic Sea to the Euxine, was originally inhabited by a race of savages known by the name of CELTS, or GAEL.....About 2160 years before the Christian era, the Scythian nomades from the north of Persia passed the river Araxes and Mount Caucasus, and settled round the shores of the Euxine. This was the first appearance in Europe of our ancestors, who in subsequent ages, and in distant countries, severally assumed the general names of Getes, Goths, and Germans, probably from their successful valor; of ALEMANS or All-men, either from a confederacy of tribes, or to express emphatically their virility; and of FRANCS or Freemen, to distinguish themselves from the slaves whom they vanquished. About 360 years after this period they began to settle in Thrace, Illyricum, Greece and Asia Minor, under many denominations; and in 300 years, or 1500 hundred before Christ, they had completed the settlement of these countries. They peopled Greece under the name of neaaeroi, or *Pelasgi*. Our immediate ancestors, then, the Jutes, Angles and Saxons, though thirteen hundred miles distant from these, being of the same race, must have had an homogeneal speech"[xxix]

To first remark upon the last sentence of the quoted paragraph

from D'Anville's preface, several of the other authors do relate to

the speech comparison and impending similarity as well between the nations; which proves to be uncanny since Emerson himself in

his journals remarks upon the very same aspect:

> We have said that the first nations
> were remembered by their religion;
> -- and in tracing down their history a
> little farther until the time of written
> languages we find that the first
> efforts which the human genius
> made to commit its ideas to
> permanent signs were exercised
> upon the great topic which stood
> uppermost in an unperverted mind."
> xxx

Since both sources of Emerson and *The Compendium of Ancient

Geography* refer to languages as being a unifying aspect to human

roots, (other sources found at the Manse say this as well,) we can

take this to be something that most took to be fact. And since it

states that not only are we as a race are all from the same original

source, from Asia, the north of Persia—but most importantly— the

German regions were settled before the Grecian ones—making this

region a more true source for ancestors of the English people than

the Greek. However, the thought that all of the present race

derived directly from Asia contradicts the mere existence of the

Celts. No author in this collection seems to have an explanation for

this—they were simply "driven out". This is confirmed with the

British Section of the Encyclopedia, in describing England:

> The earliest population of Britain is generally believed to have been Celtic. To the Celtic population of England succeeded the Gothic. The Scythians, or Goths, advancing from Asia, drove the Cimbri, or northern Celts, before them; and, at a period long preceding the Christian era, had seized upon that part of Gaul which is nearest to Great Britain, where they acquired the provincial denomination of *Belgae*. Their passage to England followed, of course,…These Belgae may be justly regarded as the chief ancestors of the English nation. The Saxons, who made the second conquest of England, were inconsiderable in numbers; nor did they exterminate the natives, but made them slaves."[xxxi]

If the Celts were also the first in Scandinavia, as the preface for Mr. D'Anville's work proposes, and the Goths drove them out there is a good chance that they also kept some as slaves. IF this be the case, then the Celts are the very first of the line of the occupants of Scandinavia, despite that all of the authors claim the "true" ancestors of the Scandinavian race be the Goths who came from Asia through Germany. This becomes important for what follows: Two specific characteristics of the Celts, or Gauls, in England as is related by Tactitus of the Roman invaders, was that they were divided into small kingdoms that were not united together, except under "extraordinary conditions" where they would come together under a common leader. They did not join bands to wage war against a common enemy. This is very similar to the tribes in the

German/Scandinavian lands at this time of the world as well.

> Little is known of the limits of regal
> authority among the ancient
> Britons; but, if that power be
> changeable in its extent even in the
> enlightened societies, how
> dependent must it have been on the
> personal character of the individual
> potentate among a people so rude!
> We have an instance of a father
> excluding his son who had offended
> him, from a share in his dominions,
> we have instances also of the
> public respect for hereditary right,
> and of its extending to female
> succession. [xxxii]

The article goes on to say that the popular opinion had a high

influence on the outcome of certain affairs, and proved to be a

powerful force. This is demonstrated in the case of Vortigern, King

of the Britons, who were incensed that the Saxons would turn

against them after assisting their cause against the Picts. "They

deposed Vortigern, who had rendered himself despicable by his

vices and by his weakness, and entrusted their fortunes to his son

Vortimer." [xxxiii] As declared in a review of *The History of the*

Common Law of England in the February, 1822 edition of the

Edinburgh Review, it agrees with the concept of how laws were

executed: "One leading principle pervades the primeval polity of the

Goths, Where the law was *administered*, the law was *made*." [xxxiv]

continuing with the possibility that the Celtic ways came through the

Gothic, it is conceivable that this was Celtic policy first. XVIII Page 111.Among the old Saxons of the continent customs & phrases are remarkable.

All of the above seems quite similar to the Scandinavian ways, in regards to dividing up a father's lands to his sons, as well as the respect for women—this seems to be an ongoing but unique Scandinavian trait, as Madame de Stael remarked earlier, and as is being shown, could be a Celtic trait, since it was a Queen who lead her Celtic tribe to implement the burning of the city of London in 61 AD. Note-worthy, too, is the mention that they picked mistletoe for their sacred ceremonies: "Mistleto, a plant produced on the branches of the oak, was gathered by them with every circumstance of awful solemnity."[xxxv]

This plant was also special to the Scandinavians, and had a specific role in the myth involving the death of one of their gods, Badlr. Therefore—it seems that some of the hereditary traits of the Scandinavians also derive from that of the Celtic Gauls, and not only from the Asian tribe led by Odin.

D'Anville's book continues to reveal another notable fact that the arrival of the Picts (also spelled Piks, or Pics) in North Britain, were originally a nation of Scandinavian Goths from Norway.[xxxvi] This becomes important because the Britons were granted help from the Saxons to wage a defensive battle against the Picts – and after a while, the Saxons realized that The Britons were in possession of quite fertile land, and so eventually sided with the Picts against the Britons. So come the years of mid 400 AD, much of Britain was inhabited with those of Scandinavian origin.

Even Mademe de Stael declared that the "particular character of the Northern literature has all derived from the Patriarch of the Celts."[xxxvii] It is noted that she lumps all of 'Northern literature' to mean that of English and Germanic lands, thus indicating either she also believed that the Celts were the original people of the Scandinavian islands—the Cimbri—and that it was hereditary, or that the Scandinavians took the Celtic literature as their model when writing their own prose. Either way the indication is there that some of the independent trait comes from the very first populations of the Scandinavian region.

All of this is important because Emerson was concerned about the issue of race, and hereditary traits. He was fascinated as to whence we as humans came from, and wanted to form ideas about the human spirit, and especially, the origin of it- which naturally would include the origin of humans themselves. If Self-reliance was the doctrine he deemed most important, then it would be in his best interest to trace the history of whence this particular trait came from. With the wealth of historical information available within his own family's collection at the Old Manse, it is safe to say he read the entire background of them as well, and pondered the conflicts presented by the various authors available to read there. The conflict between the Gauls and the Celts, or rather between the authors about the true idea of their migration, does leave one to wonder what Emerson's thoughts on the subject would be, since there are many statements on Asia and Scythians in his journals, so certainly he was aware of this idea that the originators of the "official" Scandinavian line came from Asia. However, the notion that the Celts were in place in the Northwestern lands before the Asians arrived led by Odin, and all of the traits attributed to him and his teachings, would play its part in how Emerson viewed all literature and activities that took place in these lands—thereby adding to his thirst to the ever-present question of heredity. It would also add to his curiosity how much of the marked Scandinavian trait of Self-Reliance derived from the Celts, thereby making some of the original British inhabitants born with this trait as well. However, Andrew Swinton strongly declares, "The poor Laplanders then dwelling in Sweden and Norway, were no doubt first disinherited: they still have traditions among them, of battle with those invaders; and from their manners and customs at this day, we can trace their Scythian origin." [xxxviii] If this be the case, I am wondering why there are not more inquiries into what the exact mannerisms of the Scythians are, since this seems to be one of the main agreed sources for the mannerisms for the Scandinavians. An answer cannot be determined for this at this time, but it was certainly a possibility that Emerson looked for one. Related to this topic directly or not, his idea about moving forward, literally and figuratively, is made clear by the following statement from his journals: "We know that a primitive nation never makes any considerable progress until it has first been acted upon by some foreign impulse."[xxxix]

The list at the back of Hume's book does not include the name of Odin, however I will include information on him since he is the subject of several creations of Emerson in his youthful journals , not to mention actually appearing in the essay of Self-Reliance [xl]and his existence fall right into this time, and is relevant to this study. From reading about the accomplishments and character of Odin Emerson could have gleaned much of the ways of the Scandinavian—the mind-set and activities of a pioneer, justice, ingenuity, leadership, loyalty, fearlessness, hospitality, determination. Odin also displayed the key trait of Self-Reliance—he relied on himself to lead his followers out of Asia towards the West to the Begium Sea, and North to Scandinavia. Many other Scandinavians followed his example to go west in later years – including Hengist and Horsa,

Eric the Red, who founded Greenland, and his son Lief Erickson, who later found his way to North America.

When considering the person known as Odin, one must be aware of the distinction between the mythical Odin, the Allfather of the Nordic religion, and Odin the historical figure. They are one and the same person, however the mythical adventures of Odin are not ones that are 'documented' in the literature of the Old Manse. Since the sources at the Old Manse mostly explore the historical person who led the Asian tribe into Scandinavia, I will leave the investigation of the mythical Odin for the next chapter. It should be noted, however, that in the Edinburgh Encyclopedia Section of Iceland, of which the date is obscured because the volume has, without question, more damage than any other the other volumes of the Edinburgh Encyclopedia house in the Old Manse, a somewhat brief description of the Edda of Seamund, the god of Odin, the moral code entitled *Havamal* , and a history of the Icelandic Sagas can be found.[xli] This has an impact (and obviously was followed up by other more detailed sources, as will be presented in the next chapter) since most of what is written in Emerson's journals refers to the mythical Odin, and Vallhalla, his hall in the Nordic Sky. In fact, in the first surviving journal, year 1820, Emerson was a mere seventeen years old, and there appears this unfinished poem:

> Come to my mansion house of the forlorn
> We'll have you known it was destitute & torn
> Come if you dare come when the winds are high
> Go if you will go when Geralde must die
> And summon Euphorbus Grave give up thy dead
> Think on the thunderboldt think how it sped
> When the heaven smitten Titanon bowed his head
> If thou art bolder speak thy wishes forth
> One witness shall hear from the heights of the north
> One pen shall record in the scrolls of the sky
> One *arm* shall perform which is powerful on high
> Woe to thee! woe! If the daemon fulfil
> His oath to Euphorbus of havoc & ill
> He stood on a height in (of) the fields of the air
> Sanctioned by Death; & Destiny was there
> In Odin's dread hall in the north of the sky
> He doomed the Euphorbus abandoned to die
> He summoned the dead from their coffins to come
> And shriek in thy ear their own horrible doom
> With the hosts of black hell embattled they came
> Blasted & seared with their fiendish flame
> Till the hall of the Thunderer rung with the peal
> And Nature shrunk back from his chariot wheel
> He hung out a comet to point you the way
> Which leads you to ruin" [xlii]

This poem is strongly assumed to be an original creation by Emerson.[xliii] What makes it unusual, of course, is that Euphorbus is a Greek hero of Southern mythology fame—not Nordic. It therefore strongly indicates that Emerson knew about the entire land history of Scandinavia and Britain—from the Celts to the Romans to the Saxons and beyond. This poem could easily be interpreted to have taken place in England at the time of the Roman invasion, around the period of 400 AD, since it mixes Southern and Northern elements, speaks about death, suffering and war,-- and Geralde is a name with Celtic and British origins. Without entering into a full interpretation of the possible meanings of the poem, I will certainly venture into a few ideas: "Come of you dare where the winds are high" could easily mean the highlands of Scotland, or the plains of Denmark, both of which are known for their windy landscapes; Euphorbus claimed to be reincarnated by the philosopher Pythagoras, So perhaps others had claimed to reincarnate him as well—and this would be the oath of the devil (since a pure spirit would not be reincarnated). The chariot wheel seems to be that of Odin, since he, along with Thor, is the God of the Thunder, and his hall, Vallhalla, in the north of the sky.

One more journal entry implies that not only did Emerson know about he entire history, but he contemplated it at length as well: "After the extinction of the (ea) western Empire and the settling down of the northern emigrants in the south of Europe a long period of ten centuries (compromises) is embraced under the name Middle Ages."[xliv]

Next in line and across the English channel arrive the Saxons, piloted by Hengist and Horsa, the two Saxon princes that led the Saxons to England in the year 449. They are important to document here as well, for several reasons—one because they bridge the connections of Saxons with those from the Scandinavian countries by their belief system, and because there were various sources in the Old Manse that told of their trip to England and leading the Saxons across the channel to help the Britons defend themselves against the Picts of Scotland. It is disputed if the

Saxons were actually invited over, or if the Saxons simply saw a

choice opportunity to help a weakened people, gain their trust, then

attack them themselves for their fertile lands.[xlv] The Saxons were

not so loyal to the Britons, but were certainly loyal to their own kind,

The Picts, who were, as documented above, a tribe originating from

Norway. And as David Hume claims in his book *The History of*

England in describing Hengist and Horsa:

> They were reputed, as most of the
> Saxon Princes, to be sprung from
> Woden, who was worshipped as a
> god among those nations, and they
> are said to be his great grandsons;
> a circumstance which added much
> to their authority. We shall not
> attempt to trace any higher the
> origins of those princes and
> nations. It is evident what fruitless
> labour it must be to search, in those
> barbarous and illiterate ages, for
> the annals of a people, when their
> first leaders, known in any true
> history were believed to by them to
> be the fourth in descent from a
> fabulous deity, or from a man
> exalted by ignorance into that
> character.[xlvi]

With this depiction, Hume does the reader a favor by zeroing in on

the distinction between the mythical Odin and the historical man of

Odin, without going into much detail, but nevertheless revealing

several things; that Odin-Woden- was indeed worshipped by the

Saxons, and that the man was made into an idol by the people who worshipped him; however Hume doesn't go into detail of how this particular stunt had happened. Regardless, all sources agree that brothers Hengist and Horsa were thought of to be ancestors of Odin, and so were respected for their divine lineage as well as their strength, bravery and nobility. As Emerson states in his essay *Self-Reliance*, "And truly it demands something godlike in him who has cast off the common motives of humanity, and has ventured to trust himself for a taskmaster. High be his heart, faithful his will, clear his sight, that he may in good earnest be doctrine, society, law, to himself, that a simple purpose may be to him as strong as iron necessity is to others!"[xlvii]

"Taskmaster" in my opinion, is an intentional word for Emerson to use (of course, there are many who specify that all of Emerson's words were intentional). However, when one reads the following passage regarding the Saxon Princes of Hengist and Horsa from the Section of England in the Edinburgh Encyclopedia, it becomes somewhat more than coincidence:

> Led on by Hengist and Horsa, two brothers, who were celebrated as amongst the noblest and bravest leaders of the nation, they soon finished the task in which they were called to accomplish. The northern barbarians were unable to resist their valor. [xlviii]

Some authors seem not clear if the Saxons were the same people in the Nordic countries as they were in the middle of the continent, such as the Germanic and Belgium lands, yet, in consideration of the issue above regarding Odin as ancestor to Hengist and Horsa, it is proven they had the same, or quite similar, religious aspects to their spiritual faith. According to the book *A View of the Religions in the World* by Alexander Ross originally published in 1696, "The Danes and Swedes worshipped the same gods that the Saxons did. They call upon *Thor*, or *Jupiter*, when the Pestilence is among them, because he ruleth in the Air: In the time of War they call upon *Woden*, or *Mars*."[xlix] Since Mr. Ross also explains the Gods of the Grecian religion previously, he uses them to make direct comparisons to the Northern deities for clarification. Earlier he explains that Odin "was the *German's Mars*, and is called *Woden,* from being wood, or Mad, intimating hereby the fierceness of Souldiers (sic) and fury of War."[l] From this explanation we can safely say that they were a connected people.

With regard to the Saxons being inherently brutal along with relying on their own kind to look out for their own best interests, since many of the authors then write of this being the case, Dr. Goldsmith writes in his book *An Abridgement of the History of England* published in 1813,

It was in this deplorable and enfeebled state that the Britons had recourse to the Saxons a brave people; who for their strength and valour were formidable to all the German nations around them, and supposed to be more than a match for the gods themselves. They were a people restless and bold, who considered war as their trade; and were, in consequence, taught to consider victory as a doubtful advantage, but courage as a certain good. A nation, however, entirely addicted to war, had seldom wanted the imputation of cruelty, as those terrors which are opposed without fear are often inflicted without regret. The Saxons are represented as a very cruel nation; but we must remember that their enemies have drawn the picture.[li]

Here Goldsmith acknowledges that the Saxons were reputed to be ruthless, yet admires them still for their bravery, and lack of fear due to being "addicted to war" – which would make them the type of unafraid people that Emerson describes in his self-reliance essay. As he writes, "If we cannot at once rise to the sanctities of obedience and faith, let us at least resist our temptations; let us enter into the state of war, and wake Thor and Woden, courage and constancy, in our Saxon breasts."[lii] In his journals, although for the most part deplores the whole business and putting it down as leftover from the times of the brutes, Emerson does admit to the merits of war, showing that even when he may not like it, he acknowledges that war possesses some good traits:

> When the angels of Ambition & War have sounded upon the earth, when the famished eagle screams for food and the standards of the nations soiled with blood are lifted from the dust shewing (sic) at once the proof & the promise of carnage, new sets of feelings take place in the human breast which amaze & contradict speculation. Then is exhibited the mind's power of accommodation to the tone of things, of becoming all things to all men.[liii]

With all that is written about the Saxons and their assimilations with those who lived in the Nordic lands as well as their engagements in Britain and involvements with the Britons, one thing is not mentioned: Their dependence. They were a fierce people that relied on themselves, were known for their strength and bravery, and went after what they wanted, seemingly without fear and without needing others to assist them. Once Hengist and Horsa had cleared the way, thousands more Saxons came over to the British Isles, to utilize the fertile lands there and make a better life for themselves than the Baltic coast could give them; and although Horsa was killed in battle, Hengist lived and ruled for another several decades—and founded the kingdom of Kent.[liv] It is little wonder, then that these two princes, as well as the Saxons in general were written several times on that list in the back of David Hume's book, and mentioned more than once by Emerson in his own writings.

Chronologically we move on briefly to Egbert, who was included with the year 827 beside his name in the hand-written list at the back of the manuscript *The History of England* by David Hume. He was included logically because he was the first monarch in place of a united England when the first wave of Viking Danes attacked the British shores. I will use some of the information on Egbert to demonstrate an example of some of the overlapping texts I have found in the Collection at the Old Manse. Here is how Dr. Goldsmith phrases the occurrences involving King Egbert:

> About seven years after this first attempt, they made a descent upon the kingdom of Northumberland, where they pillaged a monastery; but their fleet being shattered by a storm, they were defeated by the inhabitants and put to the sword. It was not until five years after the accession of Egbert, that the invasions became more formidable. From this time on they continued with unceasing ferocity, until the kingdom was reduced to the most distressful bondage.[iv]

While this paragraph is descriptive of the happenings surrounding Egbert's time, it is uncannily similar to the *History of England* description written by David Hume:

> The next alarm was given to Northumberland, in the year 794, when a body of these pirates pillaged a monastery; but their ships being much damaged by a storm, and their leader slain in a

> skirmish, they were at last defeated by the inhabitants, and the remainder of them put to the sword. Five years after Egbert had established his monarchy over England, the Danes landed in the Isle of Shepey, and having pillaged it, escaped with impurity.[lvi]

Either both David Hume and Dr. Goldsmith had the same primary resource to extract this information from and (assumedly) bring it to modern English standards in the same manner, or one reader was using the other. Since David Hume's work was published in the late 1700's, and Dr. Goldsmith's book is actually entitled An Abridgement of The History of England (however with a different subtitle), and not published until 1813, it would be safe to presume that Dr. Goldsmith was conducting an unofficial quite close reading of David Hume's manuscript when writing his own.

The Edinburgh Encyclopedia tells the same account, however with decidedly different phrasing:

> But scarcely had England established and regulated his (King Egbert's) infant monarchy, when a new enemy unexpectedly appeared on the coast. A swarm of barbarians from the shores of the Baltic, under the names of Danes and Normans, had filled the western countries of Europe with slaughter and devastation. Their first appearance in England was in the year 787. [lvii]

Egbert was on the throne when these attacks had begun taking place; The assumption that he is on that list is because he is a pioneering figure in being the first sovereign of the seven combined Kingdoms, and, as mentioned previously, was the first monarch to deal with the Viking Invasions. however, since he is only mentioned in the hand-written list and not in Emerson's journals, it is necessary only to acknowledge his place in the timeline.

To take a quote directly from Emerson's journals, it is necessary to include a little information about Eric the Red, who was the founder of Greenland. We know that Emerson was also an admirer of those who ventured from Norway to Iceland, then ultimately to Greenland, as he writes his own account about it in his journals:

> The Chronicles of Norway say that in the year 982, Eric the Red, a Norwegian youth of noble family sailed from Iceland with 25 ships, in quest of adventure & discovery. His fleet took a southwesterly course & came to a pleasant land full of lofty timber & of fresh & verdant vallies. Pleased with the beautiful coast, which he called Greenland, Eric resolved to settle there. After building their houses, they wasted the short summer in the pursuit of the game which was very abundant. But a summer of unusual mildness was followed by the stern winter of those high latitudes. Their harbour was frozen & the ill fated colonists beheld with despair a vast barrier of ice accumulating on the coast to

shun then out forever, from all communication with the rest of the world. They are supposed to have perished miserably with cold & famine. The Court of Denmark sent out several ships to search out the lost Colony, in vain. The sailors believe the ghosts of the settlers guard the coast & make it all the more dangerous.[lviii]

This story of Eric the Red is on the second side of a scrap of paper and attached by wax to page 52 of his journals. Obviously, he thought it was important enough to keep; whether he copied from somewhere and attached it later, or was interested to have it in his journals from a book he was studying in his room at the time, we are not to know. What this passage does demonstrate is the independent spirit of Eric the Red. Regardless of the outcome of the expedition, Eric went "in quest of adventure and discovery". This in itself made the story valuable enough to hang on to in his journals. This very same account is written in the Edinburgh Encyclopedia Section of Greenland, except they maintain that the discovery of Greenland happened several years earlier than is stated above. It begins the account, as follows:

An Icelander, Eric Raunde, or Eric the Red, so called for his red hair, having killed another powerful chief of that land, was obliged to quit the country, and determined to make a voyage of discovery, a practice very common at that time. Soon after he set sail, he reached the point of a

> cape on the continent of Greenland,
> which cape he called Heriolfsnaes,
> in commemoration of one of his
> ancestors.[lix]

Surprisingly, the account of Eric the Red in its entirety, detailed and long as it may be, does not describe the ending to the first Greenland colony that Emerson writes about. It does tell that Eric the Red boasted how wonderful Greenland was to the Norwegian population, and convinced 25 boatloads of adventurous settlers to follow him there; but gives the detail, which Emerson does not, that only 14 of these ships actually made it to the Greenland shores.[lx] This passage also gives perhaps an insight as to why this particular section was related to in Emerson's journal: It then tells the story of Eric Raude and his sons Lief and Thorstein making excursions at one time or another, and one of these trips was to the eastern coast of the North American continent, which they named Winlandia, and founded colonies there.[lxi] The other item that it mentions, which was sure to be significant to Emerson, considering his interest of the Danish role in England, was that "Greenland was always considered to be the property of Denmark, the Danish flag having been hoisted there as early as the 13th century."[lxii]

Not much else is related in the way of the Ancient Norwegians or other Scandinavians coming to Greenland, and one of the last paragraphs concerning the people of Greenland states "They have no

157

traditions from their ancestors, except an incongruous account of their battles with the old Norwegians, the history of the Greenlanders is therefore buried in impenetrable darkness."[lxiii] They are noted for their intelligence and their strength, robust and heartiness, and ingenious manner of making boots for their feet. The inhabitants discussed are the Inuit Eskimos, and left out are the European descendents of Norwegians that landed there so long ago,--there isn't much else to describe the people of the parties of colonists. The conclusion is that Emerson's sources for the activities on and of the island of Greenland must have been acquired elsewhere than the Old Manse, even though the pages for much of the section of Greenland have been cut, indicating that someone had been reading them. This will be discussed in the next chapter, since he does mention Greenland several times in his journals.

The next section of sovereigns I will cover very briefly, since it isn't my intention to delve into a history lesson, and the Scandinavian lineage within Britain has already been established. They are also the kings in place at the height of Viking activity, and this activity and interactions with the English kings will be covered in the next chapter.

Alfred is the name that comes up most in Emerson's journals. He is quite possibly the one that came into Emerson's life first, since his is the earliest Edinburgh Encyclopedia section still available at the Old

Manse: 1812. Emerson has dedicated many entries to Alfred; he writes his name singularly, together with King Canute's name, and in conjunction with other figures in history that he admired. The Edinburgh Encyclopedia complements the personality of Alfred: "The character of Alfred stands high in the records of history, and he is considered as one of the best and wisest princes that ever adorned the annals of any nation."[lxiv]

King Alfred was known for many traits, including independence, ingenuity and Self-reliance. Ascending the throne at the young age of 22 (some sources at the Old Manse say 23), he had to devise a method to keep the Danes on friendly terms with the English, so that they could all exist peacefully together on the English soil. Unfortunately, the Danes continued to break treaty after treaty, and Alfred, after countless attempts at negotiations with them, finally had to resort to hiding in the woods. After being there a year or so, he heard that the English natives had won a victory over the Danes, and so begin planning his tactics, by surprising them every once in a while without revealing who he was. Eventually, he was able to negotiate a lasting treaty with them, and ruled a peaceful England for 30 years with both Danish kingdoms and English kingdoms sharing the same British Island. "As a king, he was peculiarly eminent for his civil and his military qualities, and did everything possible for the good of the people. As a man, he set them an example of every personal virtue."[lxv] Source after source goes on to praise the merits of Alfred: "The wisdom and virtues of one man alone were found sufficient to bring back happiness, security, and order; and all the calamities of the times found redress from Alfred." [lxvi] Emerson admired much about Alfred, and especially admired his peaceful and peacekeeping policies. In the lengthy journal passage below, much of which will again be addressed in the next chapter, Emerson reveals his feelings not only about Alfred and his worth, but a bit about Sharon Turner's take on him:

> If, (as saith Voltaire) the all that is related of Alfred the great be true, I know not the man that ever lived, more worthy of the gratitude of posterity. I hope the reservation means nothing. There is not one incredible assertion made either of his abilities, his character, or his actions. Besides it was not an age, nor were Saxon monks the men, to invent and adorn another Cyropaedia. Sharon Turner, an ambitious flashing writer, & elsewhere a loon, hath done well by Alfred. His praise rests not upon monkish eulogy or vague tradition, but upon *facts*. Critics may quarrel upon the reputed foundation of Oxford; it is not at all necessary to his fame. In the first place he had the smartest man of his age for his enemy, with whom he repeatedly, constantly, & vigorously fought until he finally drove him utterly from his kingdom. *Hastings*, in despair, retired to France, & obtained some little settlement from the king, where he obscurely died. The fact,

that after his entire loss of every acre of England & every man of his armies he should be able to reproduce *ab initio* his cause & kingdom, equals the Return of Bonaparte. The skilful policy of domesticating the conquered Danes and thus lulling the opposition of those myriads which swarmed in Northumbria, and at the same time creating upon his shores a formidable bulwark to the future invasions of the sea-kings, by giving their brothers a stake in the commonwealth to defend; -- this policy was not unworthy of the profound art of Augustus Caesar. The admirable military genius discovered in his position between the two divisions of Hastings' Northmen so to menace at the same time both armies & to separate both from the East Anglians, (too ready to join the aggressions of their countrymen,) the vigilance of his patrolling bands & the strict adherence to the plan measures of *defence* (sic) alone, -- indicate his masterly generalship. An instance is likewise recorded of military skill which discovers an active invention. When Hastings went up with his ships the River Lea, Alfred then dug three new channels below, & thus drew off so much water as to leave the ships aground. He built a castle on either bank to protect his works & the Northmen were obliged to abandon their ships and escape as they best might from their strongholds in Essex. His enthusiastic attachment to learning (the more laudable as it was solitary,) his care of courts & ministers of justice, his zealous & useful piety, all these combined in so extraordinary a manner with his warlike talents, are the foundation

> of his surpassing fame, of his title to
> the surname of Great. I am anxious
> to understand fully the merits &
> honesty of the records in which he
> is transmitted to us. Asser, his
> friend and instructer, (sic) is the
> chief source. Turner says nothing
> about his authenticity. [lxvii]

Canute – the first Danish King to rule England—reigned soon after the death of Alfred, upon the death of Edmund, in 1017.[lxviii] Canute wanted the two kingdoms to become one, and did not want to experience any of the warring between rulers and peasants of various kingdoms that he had experienced as a child. To remedy this, he brutally killed each person that had ever been a traitor to him, or had been a traitor to the other side, and favoring with him—he wanted only honest and straight-forward people in his vicinity, so he exterminated the rest.

Canute –also surnamed "the Great"—executed and achieved some things that were similar to Alfred, in that he united his Kingdom, established order and a common justice system and ruled a land of peace, in relative harmony and justice. As the Edinburgh Encyclopedia explains,

> Though the beginning of Canute's
> reign was marked with severity and
> injustice, he afterwards reconciled
> the English to the Danish yoke, by
> the impartiality of his administration.
> He made no distinction between the

two nations in the distribution of justice; he restored the Saxon customs in a general assembly of the states, and thus gradually incorporated the Danes with his new subjects…The latter years of his (Canute's) life were spent in the exercises of religion. He undertook a pilgrimage to Rome, built churches, and endowed monasteries; and died at Shaftesbury, the greatest and most powerful monarch of his time, after a reign of 18 years. [lxix]

He divided his three lands to his three children, (in the Scandinavian tradition of partitioning up the lands to one's offspring) Sweyn, and Harold, from his marriage to his first wife Aifwen, and each of them received a country to rule, Norway, and England, respectively. The last son, Hardicanute, who was conceived with his second wife Emma (the widow of the late king Ethelred, and had two sons, Edward (the Confessor) and Alfred), was given Denmark to rule. Edward the Confessor was the half brother to Hardicanute , Sweyn and Harold, since he was the son to Emma, conceived before she and Canute had married. Edward the Confessor lobbied for the rule of England and eventually won, and upon his deathbed in January 1066 appointed a non-relative, Harold Godwinsson, to be his successor. It is Harold Godwinsson who had to fight the battle at York in the fall of 1066 against Harald Hadrada, the Norwegian King who wanted to take control of England, and because of that battle, Harold

Gowinsson was too exhausted and depleted of troops to win the battle against William the Conqueror after traveling 240 miles south of York to meet him on the shores of Hastings, a mere two weeks after the battle with King Harald Hadrada.

Much of the latter part of this information will be addressed again in the next section, however it is important to note that it was all available at the Old Manse as well. And as has been demonstrated above, important to the Emerson family. Alfred and Canute were especially significant to Ralph Waldo Emerson, since they were two of the very first Scandinavian-associated names written into Emerson's journals[lxx]. The trait that all of the Scandinavians—and Alfred-- that Emerson admired display is that the descriptions he read about them proved them to be problem solvers, and self-reliant ones at that. Odin, Hengist and Horsa, Eric the Red Alfred and Canute all displayed similar characteristics. They were all pioneers, in what they were doing, were leaders, and made the effort to take care of their people. All had original thoughts as to how things were to be done. Each was industrious, and displayed perseverance in their individual endevours. Odin wanted to go to a new land, and so led his people there (he also wanted to become a Deity, so he sacrificed himself to himself in order to do so. This will be addressed in the next chapter). Brothers Hengist and Horsa realized a good thing when they saw it, which was England—and so devised a way to stay in that fertile land. Eric the

Red decided beginning an entirely new colony in on a foreign island (much life Hengist and Horsa, and indeed, Odin) would be the ideal next step in his life. Alfred knew that battling the invading and settled Danes was not going to yield to a peaceful England—so he devised a method to get them under his control, then compromised with them, and ruled peacefully for 30 years. Canute was reputed to be quite brutal in the first years of his reign, but that is later proved to be so he could count on the people in his immediate court to be loyal and just, and was able to rule a Kingdom that enjoyed, for the most part, freedom from strife. Each also displayed a distinctive trait known as courage—in the case of the Scandinavian, one could call it lack of fear of death, and fear of suffering. Swinton has a passage to boast the bravery and endurance that they were so proud of among the Norwegians: ."They pique themselves on keeping cold at defiance, and to show their hardiness, they will even put snow in their bosoms." [lxxi] The Scandinavian wasn't fearful of the possibility that he might die in battle or invasion or adventure—and this made them fearless, and willing to try anything that life could offer. They were each their own champion, in charge of their own fate, and unafraid. To further emphasize the admiration Emerson had for this trait, he asks his then-contemporary 18th century readers to realize that fear cripples the strength of humanity in his essay *Self-Reliance*: "The sinew and heart of man seem to be drawn out, and we are become timorous, desponding whimperers. We are afraid of truth, afraid of fortune, afraid of death, and afraid of each other"[lxxii]

I believe Emerson felt he could learn from the Scandinavians—the ones who lived in a harsh climate, prospered, found their own way of making themselves successful—they did not model themselves after another country, or population—they were themselves the originators of their actions, and learned how to observe and absorb and incorporate other customs they believed to be advantageous. This captivated Emerson, and even though many of his journal entries show his thoughts to consider the Scandinavians of old a bit base and unrefined—I hesitate to use the word barbarous, or even savage, since Emerson seems to use these terms to refer to not only the Scandinavians, but the Greeks and at times the Native Americans as well—but a raw and unrefined of the purest essence—and later in his essay of *self-reliance*, he consistently calls to the reader to return to the base and unrefined self, to find the true essence of the human spirit lying underneath all of the layers and refinement. Some might argue this is a coincidence—I am convinced it is a direct related connection.[lxxiii]

What else was so significant in the evidence at the Old Manse in regard to this topic? And old map, with the title of the old Germany, with a date of 1843—long after Emerson was a child, and yet—the map section that was saved was the northern part—the section that shows Denmark—the rest of the map was no longer there.

One thing to note was that many of the pages that were cut—and therefore proof of being viewed, and assumedly read—was the descriptions of landscapes for each country. Why would that be significant in the quest of finding out how this was all influential to Ralph Waldo Emerson? There are several possible explanations, the most obvious would be a comparison of the landscape in the northern countries to the landscape in England. If the Scandinavians were a collective people reputed to be adaptive, self-reliant and ingenious, and could not only survive in a cold harsh unforgiving climate, but could actually thrive, to the extent that they went exploring, raiding and invading—and became one of the wealthiest and most respected sections of the world—then there must be something to be learned from how their natural environment triggered this explosion of success and prosperity. Some of the sources surely made the northern climate of Lapland, for example, sound like a more difficult situation to survive in—yet the Laplander, as formerly mentioned, discovered the means to feed and cloth himself with upmost efficiency, Another idea is that he wanted to compare the landscape of the Scandinavian countries to that of the American New England, to see if there were any similarities that could be found and therefore perhaps learn from the Nordic people the best solutions of how to survive—granted there are no reindeer in New England, however some other similarities could possibly have been present. This could be one explanation why there are so many cut pages in the sections that describe the landscapes of the Nordic countries. Perhaps Emerson wanted to compare the landscape and climate of those who had not only survived a harsh climate but had actually thrived in one, -- and he wanted to make his own judgment by reading about them. He does consider climate as affecting the difference in temperament, although he ponders as to the logical aspect of this, as he writes in his journals:

> It is difficult to assign the causes of difference in the attainments of two nations. For although the character of the species does obey the grand natural distinctions of the earth, and is found, savage at the poles, & civilized in the temperate zone, yet of nations in the same latitude, one shall be found no whit advanced in knowledge or greatness, & the other shall have arrayed itself with such spendour as to fill an hundred urns with the luster of its beams. Why is England renowned for arts and arms while an equally high latitude in Russia, and while Norway and the fine climates on North America have languished in Barbarism?[lxxiv]

The most likely explanation is offered by Madam De Stael. In the previously referenced article regarding one of her writings in the Edinburgh review, she gives her view of the distinction between the northern and southern climates, mentalities and landscapes. In her opinion, the people in the south speak about the freshness of nature, how alive the trees are, and the joys of the heart without really thinking about the dark aspects of existence, or thinking too much about intellectual things. The people in the north, however, are less concerned with their desires and more about pain. For this reason, their imagination is more alive, yet more internal and introspective. Spectacles and miracles have more of an impact on them, as nature itself has a stronger deeper impact on them, and reflects their climate, which is dark and nebulous. They are more concerned with thoughts and imagination because of this.[lxxv]

However, there is one facet Ms. De Stael neglected to remark upon, however, is pointed out by the reviewer of William Herbert's poem *Helga*. He states, "These champions of the North were the tremendous Beserkers, 'men of extra-ordinary stature and form, subject to sudden and violent attacks of passion, under the influence of which their fury was ungovernable, and their bodily strength almost supernatural.'"[lxxvi] Taking this into account, one could almost imagine that the passion of the Northern people was certainly intact, however was present at times of necessity, such as war. Then they would conjure up all the passion that they could, and used it to their advantage to win whatever they were set on to acquire or, side to win. It is possible, then to think of this as an creative and ingenious manner to use passion, and the genius of the Nordic people has been noted by some of the authors in this paper.

I will end this section with a quote by Emerson directly from his journals, that in my opinion, pulls the fascination of heritage together, and traces his perception from whence the entire idea of self-reliance stems from. One must remember, however, that his later meaning of the very last word changes in definition, and becomes more universal. With this in mind, I will let Mr. Emerson close with his thoughts:

> We have loosely traced the leading features of the early History of Religion before the covenants were given and (which is the same thing) in the nations where they were not known. The idea of *power* seems to have been everywhere at the bottom of the theology; the human mind has a propensity to refer all its higher feelings, all its veneration for virtue and greatness, to something wherein this attribute is supposed to reside. Cause and Effect is another name for the direction of this sentiment. It is felt by all. The terms of common speech, the names we give to immaterial things, all consent to this, and are qualifications of it. What is Honour, Mercy, Pride, Humility, Revenge – but sensations which have reference to intrinsic dwelling *power*? Honour is the worthiness which it gives; --Mercy, the

temperate forbearance of its exercise; Pride, the self-respect which attends its possession; Humility, the acknowledgement of its existence; Revenge, a barbarous use to which it is put. —It is shared among all beings, but in all has a limit and a beginning, on which the mind's eye eagerly fastens with an immediate attempt to trace the sources whence the subtle principle was derived. It is a great flood which encircles the universe and is poured out in unnumbered channels to feed the fountains of life and the wants of Creation, but every where runs back again and is swallowed up in its eternal source. That source is God. [lxxvii]

---

[i] Houghton, Emerson's Journals, Number 12, Wide World 9, page 40

[ii] Edinburgh Encyclopedia, 1819, Section Lapland, page 736,

[iii] Houghton, Emerson's Journals, Number 12, Wide World 9, page 40

[iv] Houghton Collection of Emerson Family printed artifacts, 1822.

[v] Travels, page 6

[vi] The Early Lectures of Ralph Waldo Emerson, page 238, etc.

[vii] Edinburgh Review, No. XLI, February 1813 page 42

[viii] Travels, page 40

[ix] Emerson, *Self-Reliance*, paragraph 35

[x] Edinburgh Encyclopedia, section Lapland, Page 737

[xi] Compendium of Ancient Geography, preface, xxii

[xii] Edinburgh Encyclopedia, 1823, Section Norway, page 520.

[xiii] Edinburgh Review, No. XIX, 1812

[xiv] Edinburgh Review, No. XIX, February 1812, page 423

[xv] Edinburgh Review, No. XLI, 1813, page 42

[xvi] "Their general adoption of the Protestant faith has tended to confirm that character...The particular character, therefore, which .Mad. de Stael has ascribed to the people of the North in general, will now be found, we believe, to belong only to such of them as profess the reformed religion." The Edinburgh Review, No. XLI, February 1813, page 42.

[xvii] Edinburgh Review, No.XLIX, ,June 1815, page 167

[xviii] Edinburgh Review, No. XLIX, June 1815, page 167

[xix] Edinburgh review, No. XLIX, June 1815, page 167

[xx] Edinburgh Encyclopedia, Section England, page 415

[xxi] Houghton, Emerson Journals, Journal 21 page 26

[xxii] Edinburgh Encyclopedia, 1823, section Norway, page 512, 516

[xxiii] Travels, page 43

[xxiv] Houghton, Emerson's Journals, College Notebook XVIII page 119

[xxv] The Wonders of Creation, page 5

[xxvi] "The dreams of Jornandes, and other authors of his benighted age, that find in Scandinavia the hive of the Gothic nations, have been for some time so fully exploded as to render further refutation inept...Pelouter, a French writer...takes I for granted that there were two original races in Europe, CELTS and SARMATIANS. The ancient Germans, the memory of whose manners he mistakes for the first; and the Franks, who communicated their name to his country, for the second...Accordingly we see Mallet, a citizen of Geneva, one of the preceptors of the Prince of Denmark and member of many academies, in his work on northern antiquities, confounding the Ancient Scandinavians with the Celts throughout. But this is less to be wondered at, as he is convicted by his translator of ignorance in the language of the people whose antiquities he discusses." Compendium of Ancient Geography, preface, page xxiii.

[xxvii] Edinburgh Encyclopedia, 1823, Section Norway, page 521

xxviii Travels, page 10

xxix Compendium of Ancient Geography, preface, xix.

xxx Houghton, Emerson's Journals, Wide World 3, page 17

xxxi Edinburgh Encyclopedia, Section Britain, page 546

xxxii Edinburgh Encyclopedia, Section Britain, page 546

xxxiii Edinburgh Encyclopedia, Section England, page 415

xxxiv Edinburgh Review, Number LXXII, 1822, page 289

xxxv Edinburgh Encyclopedia, Section Britain, page 546

xxxvi Compendium of Ancient Geography, preface, xix

xxxvii Edinburgh Review, No. XLI, 1813, page 41

xxxviii Travels, page 35

xxxix Houghton, Emerson's Journals, Wide World 3, page 26

xl Emerson, *Self-Reliance*, paragraph 41

xli Edinburgh Encyclopedia, no date (although deemed to be published approximately 1813-1815, since there is a reference to Mackenzie's 1810 article *Travels in Iceland*) Section Iceland, page 75

xlii Houghton, College Notebook Emerson No. XVII 1820, Page 23

xliii Dr. Lawrence Buell, in two e.mails addressed to me, 01/08.255 and 01/09/05.

xliv Houghton, Emerson's Journals, Wide World 3, page 16

xlv "We may therefore suppose that the suppose that the first visits of the Saxons to have been accidental, or, if they came invited, that it was only a small portion of the natives who took them into their pay. The Saxon ships, which we cannot suppose to have conveyed more than a few hundred men, arrived on the British coast in 449. The leaders of the troops were Hengist and Horsa, the fabled descendents of Woden." Edinburgh Encyclopedia, Section Britain, page 552

xlvi Edinburgh Encyclopedia, Section England, page 415

xlvii Emerson, *Self-Reliance*, paragraph 33

xlviii Edinburgh Encyclopedia, Section England, page 415

xlix A View of the religions of the World, page 108. Even though the book was originally published in 1696, this particular version has an inscription on the front cover, George L. Simmons, 28 Dec. 1841. Simmons was a descendent of the Ripley family, and much of his collection remains in the Emerson Family Archives housed in the Old Manse attic.

[i] AView of the Religions of the World, page 107.

[ii] Abridgement of the History of England, page 9.

[iii] Ralph Waldo Emerson, *Self-Reliance,* paragraph

[iiii] Houghton, Emerson's Journals, Wide World 6, page 21

[iv] In one battle near Aylesford, Horsa, the Saxon General, was slain; but Hengst being continuously reinforced by fresh troops from the continent overcame all opposition, and spread his devastations over the whole country. In his bloody career, he spared neither age, sex, nor condition; the priests were slaughtered on the altars; and the bishops and nobility were mingled with the vulgar in the common calamity. Some accepted of life and servitude under their conquerors; and others fled to the continent, and gave to their new settlement the name of Brittany. But Hengist prosecuted his conquests until he extended his authority over the counties of Kent, Middlesex, Essex, and part of Surry, which was denominated the kingdom of Kent, and was the first Saxon state established in England. Hengst fixed his royal seat at Canterbury, and, after reigning 40 years, he died about the year 488." Edinburgh Encyclopedia, Section England page 415

[v] Abridgement of the History of England, page 12

[vi] History of England, page 51

[vii] Edinburgh Encyclopedia, Section England, page 416

[viii] Houghton, Emerson's Journals Wide World 9, page 52 b

[ix] Edinburgh Encyclopedia, 1817, Section Greenland, page 88

[x] Edinburgh Encyclopedia, 1817, Section Greenland, page 88

[xi] Edinburgh Encyclopedia, 1817, Section Greenland, page 88

[xii] Edinburgh Encyclopedia, 1817, Section Greenland, page 89

[xiii] Edinburgh Encyclopedia, 1817 section Greenland, page 93

[xiv] Edinburgh Encyclopedia,1812, Section Alfred, page 396

[lxv] Edinburgh Encyclopedia, 1812, Section Alfred page 396

[lxvi] An Abridgement of the History of England, page 13.

[lxvii] Houghton, Emerson's Journals Wide World number 9, Page 5 Christmas, December 25

[lxviii] Edinburgh Encyclopedia, 1814, Section Canute, page 289

[lxix] Edinburgh Encyclopedia, Section England, page 421-422

Houghton, College Notebook Emerson No XVI page 101

[lxxi] Travels, page 43

[lxxii] Emerson, *Self-Reliance*, paragraph

[lxxiii] "The magnetism which all original action exerts is explained when we inquire the reason of self-trust. Who is the Trustee? What is the aboriginal Self, on which a universal reliance may be grounded? What is the nature and power of that science-baffling star, without parallax, without calculable elements, which shoots a ray of beauty even into trivial and impure actions, if the least mark of independence appear? The inquiry leads us to that source, at once the essence of genius, of virtue, and of life, which we call Spontaneity or Instinct. We denote this primary wisdom as Intuition, whilst all later teachings are tuitions. In that deep force, the last fact behind which analysis cannot go, all things find their common origin." Ralph Waldo Emerson, Self- Reliance, paragraph 5

[lxxiv] Houghton, Emerson's Journals, Wide World number 6, page 50

[lxxv] "Les poetes du midi melent sans cesse l'image de la fraichuer, de bois touffus, des russeaux limpides, a tous les sentimens de la vie. Ils ne se retracent pas meme les jouissances do Coeur, sans y meler l'idee de l'ombre bienfaisante, qui doit les preserver des brulantes ardeurs du soleil. Cette naturesi vive qui les environme, excite en eux plus de mouvemens que de pensees. C'est a tort, ce me semble, qu 'on a dit que les passions etoient plus vviolentes dans le midi que dans le nord. On y voit plus d'interets divers, mais moins d'intensite dans une meme pensee; or c'est la fixite qui produit les miracles de la passion et de la volonte. Les peoples du nord son moins occupies des plaisirs que de la douleur; et leur imagination n'en est que plus feconde. Le spectacle de la nature agit fortement sur enx; et elle agit, comme elle

se montre dans leurs climates, toujours somber et nebuleuse.' Edinburgh Review No. XLI, page 41.
[lxxvi] Edinburgh Review, No. XLIX, June 1815, pages 153-154
[lxxvii] Houghton, Emerson's Journals, Wide World number 3, page 2

Section five: Other Sources Until 1835
Ralph Waldo Emerson Library : Question about the three copies of the Edda of Saemund between R.W. Library and Harvard
Boston Latin School
Boston Public Library
Harvard College
Trip to Europe (including Thomas Carlyle)

Section Six: Sources from 1835 until 1841, when the Essay *Self-Reliance* was Written
Boston Lecture series, including the lecture "Traits of the National Genius"
Longfellow
Carlyle
Sharon Turner (Cont.)
Letters from Emerson's Family
Letters from colleagues

Section Seven: Conclusion
Wrap up of the inclusion of the nine virtues of Nordic mythology: Courage, Truth, Honor, Fidelity, Discipline, Hospitality, Industriousness, Perseverance, and Self-Reliance.

"There the Northern light reposes
With ruddy flames in circles bright
Like a wreath of ruby roses
On the dusky brow of Night" [R.W.E]

Elizabeth Scofield was born in Northern California and completed her master's degree in Portland, Oregon. She has worked in Western Europe, New England and in California at various universities and language schools, and currently runs her own communications business. This book describes her experiences as a master's student and Ph.D. candidate, which began in 1993. She was bestowed the title of Visiting Associate at Harvard  University for the academic year of 2004-2005, and continued conducting research on the topic of Ralph Waldo Emerson followed by several years of volunteer work at the Old Manse in Concord, Massachusetts. This is her first book.

"To Mary Moody Emerson, February? 1821

[Mary Moody Emerson, Feb 24, 1821, praises his "letters" which she could not help reading before she went to bed. Apparently, she had just received more than one letter from him; but much allowance must be made for her highly individual manner. It is quite possible that the "letters" were variously dated sections of the same MS. Her comment seems to show that he had discussed the mythology of northern Europe and, perhaps, the subject of philosophy.]"

-Rusk, Ralph L. Ed. *The Letters of Ralph Waldo Emerson Volume One.* New York, Morningside Heights: Columbia University Press 1939